FEED ME! I'M YOURS

AN AMERICAN SUCCESS STORY

It began as a modest, local publication of shared recipes and ideas, and turned into a nationwide, bestselling success practically overnight. Now *FEED ME! I'M YOURS* is the #1 COOKBOOK FOR A WHOLE NEW GENERATION OF AMERICAN MOTHERS.

Chockful of delicious, new ideas for making natural, nutritious food irresistible to the playpen and fingerpaint set, *FEED ME! I'M YOURS* tells you how to make everything from banana smoothies and peanut butter bread to yogurt popsicles and tuna burgers. A must for every mother on the brink of hot dog and French fry despair.

"Definitely a should-read book for . . . prospective mothers, new mothers, pediatricians and everyone else interested in children."
—*Pediatric Nursing*

"Well written, humorous combination cookbook and advicebook makes the job of parenting a lot easier and enjoyable."
—*Milwaukee Sentinel*

BE A MOTHER AND MORE by Joyce Slayton Mitchell
BETTER HOMES AND GARDENS® NEW BABY BOOK
CARING FOR YOUR UNBORN CHILD by Ronald E. Gots,
    M.D., Ph.D. and Barbara A. Gots, M.D.
CHILD'S BODY by The Diagram Group
CHOICES IN CHILDBIRTH by Dr. Silvia Feldman
THE COMPLETE BOOK OF BREASTFEEDING by Marvin Eiger,
    M.D. and Sally Olds Wendkos
FEED ME! I'M YOURS by Vicki Lansky
THE FIRST TWELVE MONTHS OF LIFE edited by Frank Caplan
HAVE IT YOUR WAY by Vicki E. Walton
HAVING A BABY AFTER THIRTY by Elisabeth Bing
    and Libby Colman
IMMACULATE DECEPTION by Suzanne Arms
MAKING YOUR OWN BABY FOOD by Mary Turner
    and James Turner
MAKING LOVE DURING PREGNANCY by Elisabeth Bing
    and Libby Colman
MOVING THROUGH PREGNANCY by Elisabeth Bing
MY BODY, MY HEALTH: THE CONCERNED WOMAN'S BOOK
    OF GYNECOLOGY by Felicia Stewart, M.D., Felicia Guest,
    Gary Stewart, M.D., and Robert Hatcher, M.D.
NAME YOUR BABY by Laureina Rule
THE NEW PREGNANCY by Susan S. Lichtendorf
    and Phyllis L. Gillis
NINE MONTHS READING: A MEDICAL GUIDE FOR
    PREGNANT WOMAN by Robert E. Hall, M.D.
NO-NONSENSE NUTRITION FOR YOUR BABY'S FIRST YEAR
    by Jo-Ann Heslin, Annette B. Natow and Barbara C. Raven
PREGNANCY NOTEBOOK by Marcia Colman Morton
PREPARING FOR PARENTHOOD by Dr. Lee Salk
THE SECOND TWELVE MONTHS OF LIFE edited by Frank
    and Theresa Caplan
A SIGH OF RELIEF: THE FIRST-AID HANDBOOK FOR
    CHILDHOOD EMERGENCIES produced by Martin I. Green
SIX PRACTICAL LESSONS FOR AN EASIER CHILDBIRTH
    by Elisabeth Bing
UNDERSTANDING PREGNANCY AND CHILDBIRTH
    by Sheldon H. Cherry, M.D.
YOU CAN HAVE A BABY by Sherwin A. Kaufman, M.D.
YOUR BABY'S SEX: NOW YOU CAN CHOOSE
    by David M. Rorvik with Landrum B. Shettles, M.D., Ph.D.

FEED ME!
I'M YOURS

A RECIPE BOOK FOR MOTHERS

by Vicki Lansky
with
Jill Jacobson, Stephanie Keane,
Norine Larson, Mary Popehn and Lois Parker

**Delicious, Nutritious & Fun
Things to Cook Up for Your Kids**

Illustrations by Pat Seitz

BANTAM BOOKS
TORONTO · NEW YORK · LONDON · SYDNEY

*This low-priced Bantam Book
has been completely reset in a type face
designed for easy reading and was printed
from new plates. It contains the complete
text of the original hard-cover edition.*
NOT ONE WORD HAS BEEN OMITTED.

FEED ME! I'M YOURS
*A Bantam Book / published by arrangement with
Meadowbrook Press, Inc.*

PRINTING HISTORY
Meadowbrook edition published October 1974
9 printings through May 1976
Bantam edition / February 1977
7 printings through April 1978
Updated Bantam edition / March 1979
9th printing . November 1979   11th printing ... October 1980
10th printing .. February 1980   12th printing ... October 1981

· ISBN 0-553-20719-9

Published simultaneously in the United States and Canada

Bantam Books are published by Bantam Books, Inc. Its trademark, consisting of the words "Bantam Books" and the por-
trayal of a rooster, is Registered in U.S. Patent and Trademark
Office and in other countries. Marca Registrada. Bantam
Books, Inc., 666 Fifth Avenue, New York, New York 10103.

PRINTED IN THE UNITED STATES OF AMERICA

22. 21 20 19 18 17 16 15 14 13 12

Dedication

TO PARENTS EVERYWHERE
*From those of us who have been there
and
wish we knew then what we know now*

IN THE BEGINNING ....
you'll be choosing between nursing (the original
health food) vs. formula, but at least it is two sides
of the same coin—enriched milk. The field of food
choices widens significantly by the age of six months
and for the next number of years your child's food
selection is determined mainly by you.

We have tried with this recipe book to help you with
that selection. Our recipes and ideas have been
collected with an eye towards nutrition, convenience
and fun. We hope this effort will make your task
of meal preparation and general coping with your
young infant or toddler or pre-schooler easier and
more enjoyable while he or she is keeping you
company at home.

Vicki Lansky and
Jill Jacobson
Stephanie Keane
Norine Larson
Mary Popehn
Lois Parker

Our special thanks goes to
Jeannette Stresemann Honan, R.N.,
Pediatric Nurse Associate
at the Wayzata Children's Clinic,
for her time and suggestions in
putting together this book.

Contents

Introduction

WELCOME TO THE WORLD OF THE "HAVES" . . .
children, that is, and those umpteen new
responsibilities, joys, anxieties, precious moments
and sleepless nights.

With your first child comes a new and demanding
role, that of nurturing a totally dependent person.
What you feed your child can determine his/her
mental and physical health. No one food contains
all the nutrients we need in the amounts we need,
so we must opt for a variety of foods representing
each of the four basic food groups:

> Meat, fish, poultry, eggs or other protein
>   equivalents
> Milk and dairy products
> Fruits and vegetables
> Breads and cereals

A good diet is one low in refined carbohydrates and
refined sugars. Natural carbohydrates appear in
fruits, flours, cereal and vegetables, so there is
little chance of your body not getting what it needs
if your diet is varied.

Americans are known to be overfed and
undernourished. The American diet consists of
calories far in excess of the body's needs. Refined
sugar's empty calories squeeze the nutritious foods

out of our diet. And even when we do think we're
watching our sugar intake, many of the grocery
products we buy contain hidden sugars. It is
important to become a LABEL READER! Beware of
what goes into those nice, consumer-oriented
packages. Know what you are buying. Let sugar be
part of your family's balanced diet — just not the
major part.

Nurturing means PROVIDING a balanced and varied
meal, not DETERMINING the quantities that
should be consumed. As hard as it may be to live
with at times, your small child is really the best
judge of what, or at least of how much s/he can eat.
Your attitude towards feeding will determine much
of your child's attitude towards eating. It is your
job to provide the quantity, and often the intervals.
Appetites change with growth patterns;
metabolisms are very individualistic mechanisms.
It is only when your child is old enough to
comprehend what penny candy machines provide
that you must be on guard that refined sugars and
junky foods do not push the more nutritious foods
from his or her diet.

For the full-term newborn baby, milk (mother's milk
or formula) provides the needed nutrients for the
first four or five months. Solid foods introduced
during this period are usually for the reasons of
accustoming the infant to a spoon, to new tastes,
and for providing extra satisfaction for the hungry
child. Even after that early period, milk continues
to be very important. By six months of age, it
is a good idea to start offering your baby sips of
milk or juice from a cup, regardless of whether
you're still nursing or using a bottle. It may be a
long time until your child makes the big switch
over, but it is a good idea to have the second option
open to you in times of emergencies.

If your child is still attached to his or her bottle when going to sleep after one year of age, switch the contents of the bottle to plain water at bedtime, for dentists have found that the milky film breeds decay on the back of those new little upper teeth and other research indicates that it may contribute to infantile ear infections.

The introduction of FOOD is a red letter day in your child's life though s/he will probably be neither very cooperative nor very grateful for your efforts. There is really no meal schedule as you know it, and if you feel as though your child is eating all day long, s/he probably is and is doing just fine. Be flexible; respect strong food dislikes; and

remember that

LOVE IS NOT EQUAL TO THE AMOUNT OF FOOD YOUR CHILD EATS.

FEED ME!
I'M YOURS

Baby Food from Scratch

Economy, increased nutritional awareness and a "back to nature" philosophy are some of the reasons that more and more mothers are making their own baby food. But for many parents, it is the discovery that making baby food at home is much simpler and less time consuming than they'd imagined. It can be a very gratifying experience to provide your infant with meals that save money (up to 50%), are free from additives and fillers and are fresh and as nutritious as the foods you serve the rest of your family.

Most likely you won't stop using processed baby foods altogether. So when you do purchase those little jars, read your labels carefully. Stay with the basic fruits, vegetables and strained meats. Avoid combination meals. You get less protein per serving than if you combined a jar of meat and vegetables yourself. Avoid jars containing sugar and modified starches as major ingredients. Forget the baby desserts; babies don't need them any more than we do. And when your baby has graduated to "toddler meals," s/he is definitely ready for mashed or pureed table foods.

Don't be in a rush to start your baby on solid foods. Milk (mother's milk or formula) is a more important food than solids for the first half of your baby's first year. Your doctor's recommendations and your own opinions are your best guides to what is right for your baby. Knowing when and what solids to start with is up to you. Check with your doctor before trying new foods and introduce them to baby at one week intervals to detect any source of allergic reaction.

Are you a bit nervous about making your own baby food? Start with some of the many soft or pureed grocery store foods that are available to you down the other aisles.

> Unsweetened applesauce (in the canned fruit
>   section)
> Pumpkin (canned)
> Yogurt
> Cottage cheese (may need a little extra mashing)
> Banana
> Cream of Rice cereal
> Mashed baked potato
> etc, etc, etc. . .

And when you are more comfortable with the idea, here's how to go about it safely and easily.

SOMETHING TO COOK IN

While you probably do have a pot with a lid, you may wish to invest in a steamer basket. Since many nutrients in fruits and vegetables are water soluble, they are often lost in the cooking water. This steam method of cooking best preserves the vitamins and minerals because the food is held above the rapidly boiling water and cooks in the rising steam. Steam baskets are available in most department stores (cooking area) or gourmet shops for less than five dollars. The collapsible version fits most pans. Make sure the pan you use has a tight fitting lid to keep the steam in.

Other appliances that also are helpful when cooking are: a crock pot, a pressure cooker and a microwave. No, don't go out and buy them . . . just use them if you have them.

SOMETHING TO PUREE WITH

Of course, there is your fork, but you might find it more efficient to try some of the following:

A **blender** can quickly and easily puree almost any food into the finest consistency. You will find that vegetables puree best in larger quantities and meats in smaller quantities. In general you will be using the highest speeds for the younger baby, but as s/he grows, you can proceed to a coarser consistency. Blenders are reasonably priced and useful for various other child-oriented food uses, such as making shakes, making your own peanut butter, reconstituting powdered milk or frozen orange juice concentrate. They are also good for

pureeing vegetables which can be "hidden" in meat
loaf or spaghetti sauce. Oster has special
Mini-Blend containers available which are good for
pureeing small quantities of food that do not have
to be transferred into another container.

Food processors, such as **Cuisinart,** the **Nurtury** by
Water-Pik and **La Petite** by Moulinex are all efficient,
albeit expensive gadgets for pureeing foods for
baby.

You may have or wish to buy a standard **food mill.**
These come in large or small sizes. The food is
placed in the basket and as you turn the handle,
the blade presses the food through the holes in the
bottom of the basket. The food mill strains most
cooked foods to a smooth consistency. Meat and
poultry however, will have a slightly coarser texture.

The **Baby Food Grinder** which is a small version of
a food mill has simplified pureeing small amounts
of fresh food for baby. The food fits in a well; the
turning disc is placed on top. As one turns the
handle and presses down, the pureed food comes
to the top and can be served right from the grinder.
Its small size makes it convenient to take when you
travel or eat out. It will grind fruits, vegetables and
soft cooked meats. The grinder prevents the skin
of peas and the hulls of corn (the hard-to-digest
parts) from coming through the disc when grinding.
By pureeing the food you eat, baby will be more
accustomed to the table foods s/he will soon be
eating.

And after your baby outgrows his or her need for
pureed food, you will find the
grinder convenient for:

"chopping" nuts
grinding raisins and
    other dried fruits
softening butter or
    margarine
making egg salad
mashing a banana
mashing a baked or
    boiled potato
grating soft cheeses

Baby
Food
Grinder

Baby food grinders are available in the baby departments of retail stores.

HANDLING AND STORING FOODS

Babies are particularly susceptible to digestive upsets, so it is important to remember that when you make your own baby's food proper handling is necessary. Bacteria which is present in all foods can multiply rapidly to harmful levels within hours. So as a general rule:

> Work with clean hands;
> Work with clean utensils (grinders, cutting
>   boards, etc.);
> Cook or prepare a food immediately after
>   removing it from the refrigerator;
> Freeze immediately after cooking any leftovers
>   you plan to use or "volume" foods you
>   have prepared;

Commercial baby food — the remaining unused
portion — can be stored in the refrigerator 2-3 days.
(Commercial baby food manufacturers do not
recommend using the container as a serving dish.)

METHODS FOR STORING
BABY FOOD FROM SCRATCH

When making more than just one meal's worth of
food, you need a way to store a larger volume
safely. By freezing foods, you will have the benefits
of variety and convenience of prepared foods
and you will find it easy to cook in volume. You can
always keep an adequate supply on hand and never
need to rush to prepare food for a hungry baby.

The two methods are the Food Cube Method and
the "Plop" Method:

The Food Cube Method

1) Take prepared, pureed food and pour into
   plastic "pop out" ice cube trays.
2) Freeze the food cubes quickly.
3) Pop out cubes and transfer to plastic freeze bags.
4) Label and date. Can be stored up to two
   months.

The "Plop" Method

1) Take pureed or finely ground foods and "plop"
   by spoonfuls onto a cookie sheet. The size
   of each "plop" depends on how much you think
   the baby will eat at one meal.
2) Freeze "plops" quickly.
3) When frozen, remove from sheet and transfer to
   plastic bags.
4) Label and date. Can be stored up to two months.

Do keep protein foods, cereals, vegetables, and fruits in separate containers.

Before a meal, take out the food you want to serve. Thaw it in the refrigerator or warm the food in a warming dish or in an egg poacher cup over boiling water. (Remember that cold food and milk are acceptable to your baby, even if not to you. Their taste buds are not fully developed so that warm to you may seem hot to your baby.)

As baby's appetite grows you can add more cubes per meal or make bigger "plops."

A cube or a "plop" travels well for short journeys. By the time you've arrived, baby's meal is defrosted and ready to be eaten. Food can be frozen in baby food jars. Be careful not to fill completely so as to leave room for expansion from freezing.

Small Tupperware jars with lids can serve the same purpose. They stack easily in the freezer, too.

BABY'S CEREALS

Cereals are the typical first foods given to baby because they are a good source of iron. You will find the commercial instant baby cereals both convenient and nutritious. Rice cereal is one commonly recommended first as it is easy on most all digestive tracts. But you can also easily make whole grain and unprocessed cereals such as Cream of Wheat and Wheatena. You can even run oatmeal through your blender before cooking for a finer cereal. It pays to make these cereals in quantity and freeze the balance by the methods previously described.

You may also want to try:

STEAMED WHOLE BARLEY

    1 cup whole barley
    5 cups water

Cook for approximately two hours over a low heat,
letting it steam till all the water is absorbed and the
barley is soft and fluffy. Makes 4 cups cooked
cereal.

MILLET

    1 cup whole millet
    4 cups water

Put cereal and water in the top of a double boiler
and place over direct heat. Boil for 5 minutes. Then
put top of boiler over the bottom pot which
contains water. Simmer 30-45 minutes then turn off
heat and let it steam for a while longer.

Expressed milk by a mother who is nursing added to
cereals (or any foods) may make it more readily
accepted as the smell as well as the taste are familiar
to the baby.

Any cereal can be sweetened with pureed fruits or
a bit of brown sugar or molasses.

Add a little plain yogurt to hot cereal. It gives a
creamy texture to "grainy" cereals.

For additional ideas see page 47.

BABY'S FRUITS

Except for bananas you will need to cook other
fruits till they are soft, at least till your baby is about
6-7 months old.

Banana — Use one medium size, fully ripe
(speckled skin) banana. Cut it in half and peel one
half to use. Cover the remaining half and store in
the refrig up to two days. Mash the half banana
with a fork or put it through a baby food grinder.
The riper the banana, the more digestible it is for the
baby. Ripe bananas can also be peeled, wrapped
tightly in meal-sized portions and frozen. When
ready to use, thaw and use immediately.

Apples, Peaches, Pears, Plums and Apricots —
Water Method: Wash, peel and cut fruit into small
pieces: Add ¼ cup boiling water to 1 cup of fruit.
Simmer until tender (10-20 minutes). Babies
prefer natural fruit sweetness. There is no need
to add sugar. Blend or puree until smooth. Freeze
balance.

Steam Method: Wash fruit well, remove skin and
steam for 15-20 minutes. Cool. Remove pits. Blend
or puree until smooth. Freeze balance.

Using the following recipe, you can incorporate
one of your prepared fruits into a whole meal:

COTTAGE CHEESE FRUIT

    ½ cup cottage cheese
    ½ cup fresh, raw or cooked fruit
    4-6 Tbsp. orange juice

Blend quickly and serve cool.

TROPICAL TREAT

Combine: ½ very ripe avocado, mashed or pureed
         ½ very ripe banana, mashed or pureed
         ¼ cup cottage cheese or yogurt

(continued on next page)

Canned fruits, with sugar syrup rinsed off, are also easy to puree and serve.

Make your own fruit gelatin by dissolving 1 envelope of unflavored gelatin in ¼ cup of warm water. Add 1 cup of pureed fruit and chill.

BABY'S VEGETABLES

Fresh vegetables — Use these whenever possible for best nutrition, flavor and economy.

Frozen vegetables — Best substitute for fresh.

Canned vegetables — Not as nutritious, but convenient. Already cooked; need only to be pureed. Use liquids if possible as many nutrients are in them.

Basic Recipe for Cooking Beets, Carrots, Sweet Potatoes, Peas, Green Beans and Potatoes:

Water Method: Peel and slice for fast cooking or use frozen. Cook in 1 to 1½ inches of water 20 minutes. Puree or blend with some of the cooking water or orange juice.

Steam Method: Peel and slice for fast cooking or use frozen. Steam over boiling water until tender. Puree or blend adding cooking water for right consistency.

BAKED SWEET POTATO AND APPLES

    ¾ cup cooked sweet potato
    ¼ cup liquid (milk, cooking water)
    1 cup applesauce or apples

Preheat oven to 350°. Remove skin and core and slice apples. Mix sweet potatoes and apples in buttered baking dish. Pour liquid over. Cover and bake for 30 minutes. Puree or mash with a fork.

VEGETABLE/EGG YOLK CUSTARD

    ¼ cup vegetable puree (carrots, peas, etc.)
    1 egg yolk, beaten
    ¼ cup milk
    ½ tsp. honey

Preheat your oven to 350°. Blend together ingredients and pour into 2 custard cups and place in a pan of water. Bake for 30 minutes. Refrigerate up to 3 days.

VEGETABLE SOUP

    ¼ cup cooked pureed vegetables
    1 Tbsp. butter or margarine
    1 Tbsp. whole wheat or white flour
    ¼ cup liquid (water, broth or milk)

Combine in a sauce pan till warm.

BABY'S MEATS & POULTRY

You can use any meat you have cooked for your family, or cook up a month's supply of baby food at a time, and puree it. If you want a smoother meat consistency, mix it with a cooked small serving of Cream of Rice with some milk and butter. Even a little water or juice will help the pureeing in a blender. Combine chicken with a little banana and milk to get a smooth textured meal. Meats cooked in a crock pot (minus seasonings) are tender and easy to puree.

ALL-PURPOSE MEAT STEW

    ⅓ cup flour
    1½ lbs. stew meat in one inch cubes
    2 Tbsp. oil
    3 cups water
    4 medium potatoes
    5 medium carrots
    1 - 10 oz. pkg. frozen peas

Coat meat with flour and brown in oil. Add water and cover pan tightly. Simmer 1½ hours. Scrub, peel and cube potatoes and carrots. Add to meat. Simmer 15 minutes. Add peas and simmer 5 minutes.

When pureed, this makes 4 to 5 cups.

Variation: Use any vegetable as a substitute for the potatoes, or ½ cup rice.

CHICKEN LIVER SPECIAL

    1 carrot, chopped
    1 small onion, chopped
    2 stalks celery, chopped
    ½ lb. chicken livers

Steam vegetables in a small amount of water until tender (10 minutes). Steam livers until they change color. Chop coarsely. Place vegetables and their liquid and the meat in a blender or puree in a food mill.

PINEAPPLE CHICKEN

Combine boiled or baked chicken meat in a blender with canned and drained pineapple that has been packed in its own juice. Strain the drained juice, mix with water and serve as a snack drink.

COCKADOODLE STEW

1 cup cubed chicken (or turkey), cooked
1/4 cup rice, cooked
1/4 cup vegetables, cooked
1/4 cup chicken broth
1/4 cup milk

Blend or puree together and make into food cubes or "plops."

LIVER STEW

1 cup beef liver
1/4 cup broth
1/4 cup milk
1/4 cup potatoes, chopped

Cook together until liver and potatoes are done. Puree and freeze in cubes or "plops."

Other good meat/poultry substitute meals are cottage cheese, boneless fish, cooked egg yolks, macaroni and cheese, cheese.

You will note that these recipes do not use extra salt. Studies indicate that excess salt may contribute to hypertension in later life. Salted foods are an acquired taste habit one can minimize by avoiding when possible.

YOGURT

Try it . . . You'll like it!

Yogurt is an ideal early baby food. Once your baby can take whole milk products, this should be first on your list. It is easily digestible. Any Mom "into" yogurt knows this, but what about all of you

"non-yogurt" eaters? This is an excellent time to
experiment . . . and if you don't like it, your baby
is sure to finish off the container for you.

Start with plain yogurt. It can be used as a base for
fruits (such as mashed banana) or cereals, or even
those little jars of baby food fruits. If it's too bland
for you plain, try a bit of honey in it.

Yogurt can be used in cooking instead of sour
cream or buttermilk.

Who knows, you might even like it well enough to
make your own . . . a process made super easy these
days by the new yogurt-makers on the market.

CLEAN-UP TIME

The after meal "swabbing" is seldom appreciated
by babies. You can ease the task by applying
petroleum jelly or baby oil to chin and cheeks
before a meal. Or give your little one, when s/he is
able, a damp wash cloth for a self-clean up. Most
(not all) of the food will be removed and so will
the hassle.

BEVERAGES

These beverage ideas serve as meal supplements,
snacks, or just good ideas. They can be served in
bottle or glass, for baby or toddler, and even for
Mom and Dad.

Some of these recipes call for eggs, which is a good
way of serving eggs to those children for whom
egg means, "Forget it!" Most physicians don't
recommend serving egg (cooked or raw) for babies
under six months, and sometimes even until a year,
as some young infants have an allergic reaction to
the egg white. If so, try using the yolk only, and
freeze the white for later use in baking.

Because raw eggs (the shells, actually) can be a carrier of Salmonella, they would not be a good choice for infants less than 9-12 months. Their stomachs would be much more sensitive to its effect.

While the "breast is best," the American Academy of Pediatrics recommends the use of iron-fortified formula for those using formula for up to 12 months. When your baby graduates to regular cow's milk, avoid the use of skim milk until your child is at least 2 years old as doctors feel that those butterfats in the milk are essential for young children.

NOTE: Avoid the use of honey in beverages and uncooked foods for **infants under the age of one year** as there is concern that infants can't handle certain botulism toxins that are sometimes found in honey. If these drinks aren't sweet enough with the pureed fruits, it would be better to add sugar in place of honey here.

BANANA SMOOTHIE

Blend: 1¹/₂ cups milk
              1 large banana
              1 Tbsp. honey
              ¹/₄ tsp. vanilla

Serve at once. The banana you use can also be one that has been peeled and frozen, thus giving you a way to use that last ripe banana.

SUNNY SIPPER

Blend: ¹/₂ cup honey
              ¹/₂ cup orange juice
              3 Tbsp. lemon juice
              1 can (13 oz.) evaporated milk
              1 can (12 oz.) apricot nectar

Serve chilled.

YOGURT MILK SHAKE

Blend: 1 cup plain yogurt
        1 cup orange juice
        1 ripe banana
        2 Tbsp. honey

If your little one can't quite handle apple or citrus juices, even when diluted, consider:

CARROT JUICE

1 lb. carrots (4-5 medium)
1 quart water
$1/2$ cup powdered milk

Wash the carrots and cut in small pieces or chop. Place all the ingredients in a tightly covered pot and bring to a boil. Simmer for 1 hour. Cool and strain. Serve in a bottle with an enlarged nipple hole. Store juice in the refrigerator for 2-7 days. It can also be frozen in food cubes.

Variation: In a blender combine one jar of strained baby carrots and two cups of water. Add one teaspoon of honey. Blend till well mixed. Store in the refrigerator.

MILK EGGNOG

Blend: 1 cup cold milk
         1 egg
         1 Tbsp. honey
         $1/4$ tsp. vanilla
Option: Several Tbsp. dry milk; or substitute orange juice
         for the milk.

An eggnog is also a way of providing a good protein for your older toddler who has decided to abstain from most of the protein foods you are offering.

ORANGE DELIGHT

1-2 eggs
$^1/_3$ cup orange juice concentrate
$^1/_4$ cup powdered milk
$^1/_2$ banana (or other equivalent fruit)
honey to taste
$^3/_4$ cup of water
ice

Mix in blender. The more ice you add the slushier the drink becomes.

MILK MARVELS

Add one of the following to 1 cup cold milk to add nutrition and interest. Be sure to mix well:

1) $^1/_2$ banana mashed or frozen first then mixed in blender.
2) One scoop of fruit-flavored ice cream or sherbet.
3) $^1/_2$ cup frozen strawberries plus the syrup or $^1/_2$ cup fresh berries plus sugar.
4) $^1/_2$ cup of any fresh, bruised berries, 2 Tbsp. sugar, 1 Tbsp. lemon or orange juice.
5) $^1/_2$ banana, a scoop of vanilla ice cream and 1 Tbsp. chocolate ice cream syrup.
6) Canned peaches or pears, 2 Tbsp. fruit syrup and 1 scoop of vanilla ice cream.

IMPORTANT: Remember that the protein value of milk can be increased by adding powdered milk to regular milk. But use powdered milk in moderation, especially if your child already has a low fluid intake.

DOGGIE

Finger Foods

Good health depends on sound eating habits. What your child eats and how s/he eats is established in the earliest years.

Don't Fret! Don't Nag!

Finger foods should be introduced when your child's hand-eye coordination matures to the point of being able to pick up objects and get them to his or her mouth. At approximately 6-8 months, when your child is able to sit in a high chair and can reach for objects, a graham cracker or a few Cheerios or a piece of soft cheese will be of great interest. If you allow your baby to experiment with food (despite the mess), you will have fewer problems in the long run. The more you allow your child to do, the faster s/he will learn. Don't be surprised if you need two spoons per meal — one for your child and one for you!

Be sure to supply the proper equipment: a high chair; a spoon with a bowl small enough to fit his or her mouth, and a handle short enough to control; an unbreakable cup with handles and a weighted bottom (which may save you time cleaning up the floor). Speaking of floors, you may want to use newspapers or a plastic tablecloth under the high chair to save you the 3x a day clean up.

A child needs far less food than many parents expect. A child eats when hungry, and will take just what is needed to maintain his/her growth rate. Servings should be small so as not to be discouraging . . . so should the plates or bowls. Add new foods gradually. If your child should reject a particular food, return to a favorite and then in a few days offer the new food again. It isn't always easy to respect your child's strong food dislikes, but it is important to try.

Some children cling to the personal service of being fed, but ultimately (given the opportunity) all learn to feed themselves. Food is a great self-reinforcer.

FINGER FOODS NOT RECOMMENDED
FOR CHILDREN UNDER 12-18 MONTHS

Difficult to Digest	**May Cause Gagging**
Corn	Nuts
Leafy vegetables	Popcorn
Cucumbers	Raisins
Bacon rind	Olives
Baked beans	Hard candies
Chocolate	Raw carrot sticks
Onion, uncooked	

Nuts and popcorn are **not** recommended even for older toddlers! Some children are more susceptible to gagging than others. (See page 148.)

Serve toast sticks and bread sticks with caution to very young children. Also, peanut butter should be used sparingly or thinned with milk for very young children so it will not stick in the back of the mouth and cause gagging.

Your child develops tastes during the first few years that will carry on through later life. By avoiding heavily sugared or salted foods, you can forestall and possibly prevent a craving for unnecessary foods.

Now that you know what finger foods to avoid or serve with care, here are several lists of ideas for foods that children can handle as they grow older.

FOODS APPROPRIATE FOR BABIES
6 TO 8 MONTHS OLD

Mashed bananas or small slices
Applesauce
Canned pears and peaches
Cooked cereals
Cheerios
Toast, lightly buttered
Graham crackers
Arrowroot cookies
Mashed potato
Soft cooked vegetables, mashed
Cottage cheese
Yogurt
Pudding
Vanilla ice cream
Frozen yogurt

Chicken liver and other tender meat, mashed or
    chopped
Ground meat (may or may not be accepted)

FOODS APPROPRIATE FOR BABIES
9 MONTHS TO A YEAR

Offer foods that the child may pick up.
Texture becomes of great interest at this point.

> Apple peeled and cut into eighths
> Orange sections, peeled and loose membrane
>   removed
> Peaches, ripe and peeled
> Egg, boiled, scrambled or poached
> Cheeses, soft
> Soft custards
> Carrots and other vegetables, cooked soft
> Macaroni pasta
> Egg noodles
> Rice
> Toast
> Bagel
> Tender meats; lamb, veal and some beef
> Spaghetti with meat sauce
> Fish, without bones (also Gefilte Fish)
> Tiny meatballs
> Soft cooked pieces of chicken

Most babies with 2-4 teeth, are more receptive to
lumpier foods. Regardless of age, babies do not
need teeth to chew, gums do an adequate job on
soft foods. More chewy fruits and vegetables should
be added as more teeth erupt. It is easy to drift
into the habit of serving only soft fruits and
vegetables and to perpetuate such practices as
peeling apples, but it is wise to *gradually* increase
the chewy foods as the chewing ability increases.

FINGER FOODS APPROPRIATE FOR BABIES ONE YEAR AND OLDER

Vegetables

Carrot sticks (large)
Cauliflower
Cherry tomatoes, halved
Tomatoes, peeled
Mushrooms
Lettuce, cut up
Avocado, ripe
Asparagus tips
Broccoli tips
Green beans
Cooked sweet potato
Mashed potatoes
French fries
Peas (uncooked, frozen ones too!)
Celery, with all strands removed
Pickle spears

Dairy

Small squares of soft cheese, American, Gouda, etc.
Deviled eggs made with mayonnaise
Hard cooked eggs
Cottage cheese (add fruit, fresh or canned, for interest)
Yogurt (may be served semi-frozen)

Fruit

Apples, peeled
Pears, peeled
Peaches, peeled
Navel oranges, peeled and sectioned

Mandarin oranges, canned
Fruit cocktail, canned
Fresh berries
> Strawberries, halved
> Grapes, halved for young toddlers
> Sweet cherries, pitted
> Blueberries
Watermelon, pitted and cut into bite-sized pieces
Cantaloupe, cut into bite-sized pieces
Banana, whole or cut into thirds
Dried fruits

Meats

Small meatballs
Tender roasts (may grind)
Hamburger (try it in different shapes, such as sticks)
Lamb chops (but with a bone with no sharp points)
Veal
Chicken or turkey, diced
Ground turkey cooked like hamburger
Chicken or beef liver
Tuna fish
Spareribs, well cooked
Crisp bacon*
Fresh frankfurters*
Ham, cut into bite-sized pieces*
Luncheon meats*
Sausage*
Beef jerky*

---

* These meats contain sodium nitrates (which act as a preservative and coloring agent) and they should be served in moderation as some experts question the safety of nitrates.

Breads, Cereals, Etc.

> Lightly buttered toast, cut into fourths
> Arrowroot cookies
> Zwieback
> Saltines
> Triscuits
> Pretzel rods
> Potato chips made from dried potato granules
> Oyster crackers
> Graham crackers
> Bagel and cream cheese
> Cold cereals* (dry or with milk)
> Hot cereals (regular or instant)
> Cooked macaroni (a variety of shapes)
> Cooked spaghetti
> Spinach noodles (those green ones)

Even sandwiches broken into pieces are often acceptables. It's worth a try.

As your child's ability with a spoon increases, so should the bowl-type food you serve. Be patient and try not to let the lack of neatness dissuade you from continuing his or her practice.

TEETHING

This early life passage may be quiet or traumatic. Try stale bagels, a frozen banana on a stick, the hard core of a pineapple, a frozen food "cube" on a stick, a large clean raw carrot, etc.

---

* Avoid those that are sugar-coated, honey-coated or chocolate-flavored.

Recipes for Teething Biscuits and Crackers

You can harden almost any bread by baking it in a very low (150-200°) oven for 15-20 minutes. Your baby will enjoy teething on the variety of hard breads — whole wheat, rye, etc. — that you can make this way. But you may also like to try some of the following for the economy and nutrition.

HARD ROUND TEETHING BISCUITS

> 2 eggs
> 1 cup sugar
> 2-2½ cups flour (white, whole wheat or a
>   combination)

Break eggs into a bowl and stir till creamy. Add sugar and continue to stir. Gradually add enough flour to make a stiff dough. Roll out between two sheets of lightly floured wax paper to about ¾ inch thickness.

Cut in round shapes. Place on a lightly greased cookie sheet. Let it stand overnight (10-12 hours). Bake at 325° until browned and hard. This will make about 12 durable and almost crumb-free teething biscuits.

ENRICHED TEETHING BISCUITS

> 1 egg yolk, beaten
> 2 Tbsp. honey
> 1 Tbsp. molasses
> 1 tsp. vanilla
> 1 cup flour (white and/or whole wheat)
> 1 Tbsp. soy flour
> 1 Tbsp. wheat germ
> 1 Tbsp. powdered milk

(continued on next page)

Blend egg yolk, honey, molasses and vanilla then add
dry ingredients. The dough should be stiff. Roll out
dough thinly and cut in finger length rectangles or
desired shapes. Bake at 350 degrees on an
ungreased cookie sheet for 15 minutes. Cool and
store in an air tight container. Makes 3 dozen.

BANANA BREAD STICKS

> 1/4 cup brown sugar
> 1/2 cup oil
> 2 eggs
> 1 cup mashed banana
> 1 3/4 cups flour (whole wheat and/or white)
> 2 tsp. baking powder
> 1/2 tsp. baking soda

Combine ingredients and stir only until smooth.
Pour into a greased loaf pan. Bake about 1 hour or
until firmly set at 350 degrees. Cool, remove from
pan and cut into sticks. Spread out on a cookie sheet
and bake at 150 degrees for 1 hour or longer until
the sticks are hard and crunchy. Store in a tightly
covered container.

OATMEAL CRACKERS

> 3 cups oatmeal
> 1 cup wheat germ
> 2 cups flour
> 3 Tbsp. sugar
> 3/4 cup oil
> 1 cup water

Combine ingredients and roll onto two cookie
sheets. Cut into squares. Bake 30 minutes at 300° or
until crisp. Be sure to roll thin and bake well.

HOMEMADE GRAHAM CRACKERS

     1 cup graham or whole wheat flour
     1 cup unbleached flour
     1 tsp. baking powder
     1/4 cup margarine or butter
     1/2 cup honey
     1/4 cup milk

Combine flours, baking powder. Cut in butter or margarine until consistency of cornmeal. Stir in honey. Add milk to make a stiff dough.

     Roll out on floured surface to 1/4" thickness. Cut into squares. Prick with a fork. Brush with milk. Bake at 400° on ungreased baking sheet for 18 minutes or until golden brown. If rolled thicker, these crackers can be used as teething biscuits.

Dessert Idea: Crumble one graham cracker in a bowl. Add a spoonful of honey and a bit of warm milk. Mash, mix and serve.

Toddler Food

Even though your toddler is now on "table foods" you will probably notice that your meals are more often geared towards what your child will eat than the other way around. Save your gourmet delights for a few years yet.

Children have been known to survive eating only peanut butter and jelly sandwiches (or whatever) for extended periods of time. But if you're simply out of ideas, you may want to consider some of the following:

28

LUNCH IDEAS

Deviled Ham — on graham cracker or whole wheat bread.

Cream Cheese — on graham crackers is very popular.

Egg Salad — add mayonnaise for desired consistency; very finely chopped (or grated) celery may be added.

Full of Baloney — fill slices of baloney with cottage cheese or spread with cream cheese and roll.

Chicken Salad — cubes of chicken mixed with mayonnaise, finely chopped celery and grated carrot.

Triangle Sandwiches — spread whole wheat bread with raspberry jam and top with thin slices of banana and cut sandwich into triangles, i.e. fourths.

Cottage Cheese Salad — combine 1 can crushed pineapple, 1 cup cottage cheese, whipped Dream Whip and (3 oz.) lime jello (either ½ jelled or simply sprinkled on).

Peanut Butter — for toddlers should be thinned with milk or orange juice. Spread thinly. Try honey instead of jam.

French Toast — may also be made with orange juice or condensed soup substituted for the liquid.

Cream Cheese and Cucumber Sandwich — add peeled and finely chopped (or grated) cucumber to cream cheese, then spread.

Tuna Fish Salad — mash with a fork or put in a blender (depending on desired consistency), mix with mayonnaise.

Leftover Meat Sandwiches — in a blender place about ¾ cup cubed meat, 1 hard boiled egg, 1 Tbsp. butter and 1 Tbsp. milk. This will make a paste. Keep in an airtight container in the refrigerator.

Grilled Cheese Sandwich — place 1 to 2 pieces American cheese between two slices of bread and brown in 1 Tbsp. of margarine in a skillet pan, then turn to brown other side.

Deviled Eggs — add a face by using raisins for eyes, nose and mouth.

(For additional ideas see page 137.)

Slicing a piece of bread (frozen is easiest) into two very skinny slices can make a sandwich easier to handle when hands are still very small.

DINNER

One of dinner time's biggest problems is that your child's stomach is inevitably one half hour to an hour ahead of your meal schedule. You can feed your child early and avoid the next hour's headache or try one of the following if you are determined that the whole family will eat together.

Offer a salad (or side dish) as an "appetizer." Or a carrot. An ice cube can occupy a child for a fairly long time. Serve it in a plastic cup.

Sugarless gum or bubblegum may work for you.

(Regarding gum, the concept of chewing vs. swallowing begins about 18 mos., though you'll "lose" many pieces before the idea catches hold.)

And do you find that your child simply can't sit still during the meal? S/he must stand, bounce, climb, kick the table, go to the toilet and generally drive you bananas. We can offer no remedy — only sympathy, for you are not alone. (We probably performed these same foul deeds as kids ourselves.)

Macaroni and Cheese — your combo or your grocer's. An all time favorite.

Tiny Meatballs — add beaten eggs, oatmeal or wheat germ and grated cheese.

Meat Loafies — same additions as above, but cooked in a muffin tin. (Freezes well in this form —reheat on a cookie sheet in oven or toaster oven.)

Chicken Livers — saute in butter until tender; cut into pieces. Or wrap in bacon and broil.

Boned Fish — use only fish that is quite fleshy, such as cod. Always check carefully for bones.

Corned Beef Hash — place in a frying pan. Make a depression with the back of a spoon and break an egg into it. Cover and heat until egg has settled. Messy with fingers, but not bad with a spoon.

Pineapple Franks — split frankfurters and fill with drained pineapple; broil for 5 to 10 minutes. Older toddlers enjoy these.

Omelet — whether your child likes this plain or with such additions as onions, green pepper, cheese, wheat germ, etc., it should be cooked as a large pancake rather than scrambled. It is much easier for a child to eat this when it can be broken into pieces.

TUNA BURGERS

> 1 can (7 oz.) drained tuna
> 2 Tbsp. chopped onion
> 2 Tbsp. chopped pickle
> 1/4 cup mayonnaise
> Optional: slice of cheese

Combine ingredients. Split and toast hamburger
buns, and spread bottom half with tuna mixture. Top
with 1 slice of cheese and broil for 4 minutes or
until cheese melts. Add bun toppers.

TUNA PATTIES

> 2/3 cup Grape Nuts
> 1/2 cup milk
> 1 cup finely chopped onion
> 1 Tbsp. shortening
> 2 cans (7 oz. each) tuna, drained
> 2 eggs, slightly beaten
> 1 tsp. lemon juice
> 1 Tbsp. shortening

Add cereal to milk; set aside. Sauté onions in 1
Tbsp. shortening until tender but not browned. Add
to cereal mixture the tuna, eggs, and lemon juice.
Blend thoroughly. Form 12 patties. Brown on both
sides in 1 Tbsp. shortening.

SALMON SOUFFLE

> 1 can (16 oz.) salmon
> 1 can (7 3/4 oz.) evaporated milk
> 3 Tbsp. butter
> 3 Tbsp. flour
> 1/2 tsp. dry mustard
> 4 eggs, separated
> Optional: 1 tsp. Worcestershire, paprika

Drain salmon liquid into 8 oz. measuring cup and add enough milk to make 1 cup. Pick over and flake salmon. In a saucepan, melt butter and blend in flour and dry mustard. Gradually add milk and cook, stirring until thickened. Remove from heat, stir in beaten egg yolks, Worcestershire and salmon; cool. Beat egg whites until stiff and fold into mixture. Pour into buttered 2 quart souffle or casserole dish and bake at 350° for 45-50 minutes. Dust with paprika.

LOAFER'S LOAF

1 lb. ground beef
1¼ cups oatmeal, uncooked
½ tsp. celery salt
1 cup milk
⅔ cup chopped tomatoes
¼ cup minced onion
1 egg, beaten
¼ cup grated American cheese

Combine all ingredients. Pack into a greased loaf pan. Bake at 350° for 1 hour and 10 minutes.

MEATBALL CASSEROLE

1½ lbs. ground beef
1 cup condensed tomato soup
1 Tbsp. flour
2 Tbsp. margarine
1 large onion, chopped
2 cups diced celery
4 medium potatoes, peeled and diced

(continued on next page)

Mix first four ingredients. Shape into 1½" balls
and brown in margarine. Put into casserole. Mix
remaining ingredients. Arrange on top of meatballs.
Cover and bake at 350° for 50 minutes. (May be
frozen.)

ORANGE CHICKEN

2 chicken legs and thighs
2 Tbsp. melted butter
½ cup orange juice
Poultry seasoning

Place chicken in small baking dish and season. Mix
melted butter with orange juice. Pour over chicken.
Sprinkle with poultry seasoning. Bake 15 minutes
at 350°. Turn and baste with juice mixture. Broil
for 15 minutes or until chicken is crisp and tender.

CHICKEN QUICHE

1 unbaked 9" pie shell
½ cup diced chicken
1½ cups shredded Swiss cheese
3 eggs, slightly beaten
1½ cups milk
2 Tbsp. Parmesan cheese, grated

Place chicken in pie shell and add Swiss cheese.
Combine eggs and milk. Pour over cheese. Sprinkle
on Parmesan cheese. Bake at 375° for 30-35 minutes
or until a knife inserted comes out clean. Allow to
stand 10 minutes before serving.

SIMPLE SOUFFLE

> 1/4 cup margarine or butter, melted
> 1/4 cup flour
> 1 cup milk
> 4 eggs
> 1/4 tsp. cream of tartar
> Optional: 1 cup of shredded Cheddar, Swiss or
>   Mozzarella cheese

Melt margarine, stir in flour. Cook over medium heat until bubbly. Add milk and stir constantly till smooth and thickened. Beat 2 egg yolks until smooth. Into the yolk mixture blend a little of the hot mixture; return yolk mixture to saucepan and blend. Remove from heat. Pour into 1 1/2 quart casserole. Beat 4 egg whites until stiff, not dry, along with cream of tartar and fold into casserole dish. Bake at 350° for 30-40 minutes. Delicious even when it falls!

If using cheese, add after flour and milk has thickened.

SIMPLER SOUFFLE

> 1 can condensed Cheddar cheese soup
> 6 eggs, yolks and whites whipped separately

Combine beaten egg yolks and cheese soup in a casserole dish. Fold in egg whites. Bake at 400° for 40 minutes or till done.

TASTY VEGETABLES

"If it's green, it must be yucky" is a philosophy you might run into (like a stone wall). Just increase the variety of fruits in your menus until your child's taste tolerance widens.

One way of introducing your child to new tastes, such as an artichoke, is by *not* serving it to him/her. "Adults-only" food often becomes more desirable when treated as forbidden fruit. You can "perhaps" let your child have a taste from your plate. Graduating to "adult" foods makes children feel more grown-up and at the very least saves you from throwing out or arguing over some tasty part of your meal.

One method of using up any leftover cooked vegetable is to mash it, mix it with an egg and cook it like a pancake or bake it in a muffin tin.

Older toddlers are often fond of frozen green peas straight from the freezer bag! Or try Chinese pea pods — they are sweet.

Often, too, vegetables that your child picks from your summer garden will be eaten, while the same item from your refrigerator will be passed over.

If you're really desperate, try green noodles. (They're made with spinach.)

Meat loaf and spaghetti sauce can "hide" pureed vegetables added in moderate amounts. You might even want to try this with hamburgers.

Raw vegetables often meet with less resistance than those that are cooked. Combine this with the way your toddler attacks the hors d'oeuvres when your company is starting on cocktails and you have to come up with:

RAW VEGETABLES SERVED WITH A DIP

Vegetables can include carrots, celery, cauliflower, radishes, cucumber spears, etc., etc., etc. The dip can have as a base yogurt, sour cream or cheese.

BUNNY FOOD

Combine grated carrots with raisins. Blend together
with some mayonnaise, or a bit of honey and lemon
juice.

BAKED BANANAS

Peel firm bananas and place in a well greased
baking dish. Brush with butter and bake at 350° for
12-15 minutes. Remove from oven. With the tip
of a spoon make a shallow groove the length of the
bananas and fill with honey.

HONEYED CARROTS

3 Tbsp. butter
4 cups sliced carrots
3 Tbsp. orange juice
1/4 tsp. ginger
4 Tbsp. honey

Combine all ingredients in a saucepan and cover
and cook over a low heat for 30 minutes or until
tender. Stir occasionally. Leftovers may be frozen.

NUTTY CARROTS

5 cups 3-inch carrot sticks
1 1/2 cups water
1/2 cup melted butter or margarine
2 tsp. honey
2 Tbsp. lemon juice
1/2 cup chopped walnuts (or maybe pulverized in a
    blender)

Steam or cook carrots in water until tender.
Combine balance of ingredients, except for nuts,
and heat. Pour this mixture over drained carrots.
Toss walnuts on top.

GREEN BEAN BAKE

    2 pkgs. frozen whole green beans
    1 garlic clove sliced (optional)
    1 cup sour cream
    1/4 tsp. pepper
    2 Tbsp. butter
    1 cup soft bread crumbs

Cook green beans with garlic following label
directions. Drain. Place in baking dish. Stir pepper
into sour cream and spoon over beans. Melt butter
in small saucepan. Add bread crumbs and toss.
Sprinkle over sour cream. Bake at 350° for 20
minutes.

Snacks

Snacks are a way of life in most American households. It need not be a dirty word — nor need it be JUNK! Fruits and vegetables are the most obvious snack foods, plus most of the finger foods listed in the previous chapter. Snacks, junky ones, push the nutritious foods out of our diet, contribute to tooth decay and add on pounds.

39

Do include peanuts and popcorn as a snack for your
"beyond toddlerhood" child if you feel s/he knows
how to chew them well.

Raisins (and other dried fruits) have recently fallen
from favor in the dental community as they consist
of sugars, albeit natural, that stick between teeth
and promote tooth decay. Why not consider moving
dried fruits into the main mealtime, rather than
just as a snack?

**MAGIC FINGER JELL-O: it disappears before your very
eyes.**

> 2 envelopes unflavored gelatin
> 1 (6 oz.) pkg. Jell-O or 2 (3 oz.) pkgs.
> 2½ cups water

Dissolve unflavored gelatin in one cup of cold
water. Set aside. In a saucepan, bring 1 cup of water
to a boil and add Jell-O. Bring to a boil and remove
from heat. Add gelatin mixture. Stir and add ½ cup
cold water. Pour into a lightly greased pan and
set in the refrigerator until solid (about 2 hours). Cut
into squares (or use a cookie cutter) and store in
an airtight container in the refrigerator.
    Or avoid using commercial Jell-O altogether
by combining 3 envelopes of unflavored gelatin
with one 12-oz. can of frozen juice concentrate and
12 oz. of water. Soften the gelatin in the thawed
juice and bring the water to a boil. Add the
juice/gelatin mixture to the boiling water and stir
till gelatin is dissolved. If the juice needs extra
sweetening, add it here. Follow directions for
chilling as in above recipe.

APPLES IN HAND

Peel (optional) and core a whole apple. Mix peanut butter with one of the following: raisins, wheat germ or granola. Stuff this into the hole of the cored apple. This may be sliced in half for table serving or serve the apple half on a popsicle stick. It's both novel and neat that way.

STUFFED CELERY

Remove the strands* from celery and stuff with cream cheese or peanut butter. Raisins may be added on the top of the spread.

GRINDER SNACKS

Grind figs, dates and raisins in equal amounts. (Nutmeats optional.) Add a small amount of lemon juice to a cup of graham crumbs. Make small balls out of your ground mixture and roll in crumbs for coating.

Your baby food grinder can come in handy here.

PEANUT BUTTER BALLS

$1/2$ cup peanut butter
$3 1/2$ Tbsp. powdered dry milk
A bit of honey

Combine ingredients, roll into balls and store in refrigerator. Optional additions: raisins, nuts, coconut, wheat germ, sunflower seeds, brown sugar for rolling.

---

* Optional depending on age and chewing ability of child.

GOODIE BALLS

Combine: 1/2 cup peanut butter
        1/2 cup honey
        1/2 cup instant cocoa or carob powder
        1 cup peanuts or soy nuts
        1/2 cup sunflower seeds
        1 cup toasted wheat germ
        Coconut

Roll into balls and roll in coconut. Refrigerate if
using a refrigerated brand of peanut butter, which
would be preferable.

CHOCOLATE-PEANUT BUTTER STICKS

8 oz. semi-sweet chocolate
6 Tbsp. peanut butter
1 tsp. vanilla
1 cup toasted wheat germ

Melt chocolate and blend with peanut butter and
vanilla. Stir in wheat germ. Press into a buttered
8" square pan and chill till firm. Cut into bars and
store in a container in the refrigerator.

UNCANDY BARS

1 loaf of bread (white, whole wheat, etc.)
1 pkg. peanuts, chopped
1 cup peanut butter
peanut oil
Optional: 1/4 cup toasted wheat germ

Trim the crust from the bread. Cut bread slices in
half. Put the bread and the crusts on a cookie sheet
overnight in the oven till dry or turn on oven to
150° for a half-hour or till dry. Put the dried crusts
in a blender till finely crumbed. Combine crumbs
with chopped nuts. Add wheat germ, if using. Thin

the peanut butter with oil. Spread or dip the bread
in the peanut butter. Then roll them in nut/crumb
mixture. Dry them on a cookie sheet. Store in an
airtight container. No need to refrigerate if you are
using shelf-stable peanut butter. Variation: If
candy isn't candy to you without chocolate, add a
tablespoon of instant cocoa to the thinned peanut
butter.

CHEESY WHEATS

    4 cups spoon-size shredded wheat
    1/2 cup (stick) margarine
    1 cup shredded cheese (Cheddar, etc.)

In a large saucepan, melt margarine. Add cheese.
When the cheese begins to melt, add shredded
wheat. Toss to coat well. Refrigerate if not to be
eaten within an hour or two.

CEREAL STICKS

    1/2 cup butter or margarine
    1 cup sugar
    2 eggs
    1 tsp. vanilla
    2 1/2 cups flour (white or half white, half whole
        wheat)
    1/4 tsp. baking soda
    1/2 cup plus of cereal (Grape Nuts, granola, wheat
        germ, etc.)

Blend all the ingredients plus 1/4 cup of the cereal
together. If the dough is too soft, add more flour.
Take a small piece of dough and roll into a stick
(snake) and then roll the stick in the extra cereal to
coat. (Employ anyone experienced with play dough
in your family.) Place on a lightly greased cookie
sheet and bake at 400° for 8 minutes or till slightly
browned.

SUPER COOKIES

> 1½ cups oatmeal (or Swiss Familia)
> ½ cup non-fat dry milk or Tiger's Milk
> ½ cup wheat germ
> ¾ cup sugar (or ½ cup honey)
> 1 tsp. cinnamon
> ⅓ tsp. cloves
> ½ cup oil or melted butter
> 2 eggs, beaten

Mix all dry ingredients. Add melted butter and beaten eggs. Spoon onto greased baking sheet. Bake at 350° for 12-15 minutes.

BITE OF APPLE COOKIES

> ½ cup margarine
> 1 cup brown sugar
> 2 eggs
> 1½ cups flour
> ½ cup uncooked oatmeal
> 2 tsp. baking soda
> ½ tsp. cinnamon
> ¾ cup wheat germ
> 1 cup finely chopped, peeled and cored apples

Cream shortening; add sugar and eggs. Mix dry ingredients and combine with creamed mixture. Add apples. Drop spoonfuls on a greased cookie sheet. Bake for 10-15 minutes at 350°.

NUTRITIOUS BROWNIES

> ¼ cup vegetable oil
> 1 Tbsp. molasses
> 1 cup brown sugar
> 2 tsp. vanilla
> 2 eggs
> ½ cup broken pecans or walnuts
> 1 cup wheat germ
> ⅔ cup powdered milk
> ½ tsp. baking powder
> ¼ cup dry cocoa or 2 squares (2 oz.) unsweetened
>   baking chocolate

Mix together all Ingredients except the dry milk, baking powder and dry cocoa. (If using squares of chocolate, melt in a double boiler and add here.) Sift the dry milk, baking powder and cocoa through a sieve into the other ingredients and stir well. Spread in a very heavily greased 8x8" pan and bake for approximately 30 minutes at 350°. Turn out of pan immediately and cut into bars while still warm.

OATMEAL BARS

    2 cups oatmeal, uncooked
    ¾ cup brown sugar
    ½ cup (1 stick) butter or margarine
    dash of soda

Boil sugar, shortening and soda. Add oatmeal and blend. Spread mixture in a well greased 8" square pan (or equivalent) and bake at 350° for 10 minutes. Cut in bars while warm.

FRUIT ROLL

Use apples, peaches, pears or nectarines to make this yummy dried "candy." The fruit can be the "too-hard-to-eat" variety or the "too-ripe-and-the-last-piece" variety. It even works on canned fruit which is well drained. Use mashed or pureed fruit. Two methods work well. FIRST is the blender way. Peel and core fruit, blend till smooth, then cook 5 minutes in a saucepan over moderate heat. SECOND is the freeze-defrost method. In advance, peel and core fruit and place it wrapped in the freezer. Remove from freezer an hour before using so it can start to defrost. Cook in a saucepan, mashing with fork as you go. Cook for 5-10 minutes. If very watery, drain. While cooking add 1 tsp. honey for each piece of fruit you are using. (Cook the different fruits separately, though you can cook 1 piece or a dozen of the same type at one time.)

(continued on next page)

Lay out clear plastic wrap (or cut open small plastic bags) on a cookie sheet or broiling tray. Use one piece for each piece of fruit you have cooked. Spoon mixture onto the wrap staying away from its edge. Spread as thin as possible. If you spread another piece of plastic wrap over the mixture and press down with a wide spatula, it helps to make it evenly thin. Be sure to remove this top sheet of plastic before drying.

Place your tray in the oven (at night, we suggest) which is turned on to its lowest possible heat or with just the pilot light on, and leave overnight (6-8 hrs.). The plastic wrap will not melt! If it is dry by breakfast, remove from the oven (if not, wait a while longer) and roll up the plastic wrap (with the dried fruit) as if it were a jelly roll.

THEN — PEEL AND EAT!

It will last several months this way — if your children don't discover it, that is. If you don't understand how this should look, stop in at a health food store and ask to look at their fruit roll, and the price of it!

Variation: Simply core and peel an apple. Slice it into thin "rings" and dry it as for fruit roll.

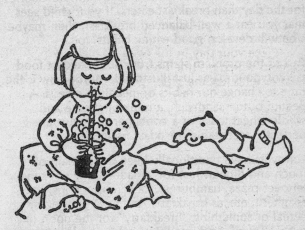

Pizza for Breakfast?

It's 7:45 in the morning. Your husband needs to leave for work by 8:15 and he's in the kitchen starting to fry up some eggs. You're giving your 3 month old milk and the 3½ year old, Chris, doesn't want any old fried eggs but would rather have leftover pizza for breakfast. Dad says, "No, pizza isn't breakfast food, and here's a nice piece of toast with jelly." You finish feeding and changing baby, give Chris some cold cereal with milk and sugar plus a glass of orange juice and then you relax with a cup of coffee or tea. You guess you'll have something to eat around 10:00 A.M. Sound familiar?

No one wants to be creative at 7 A.M. but breakfast is a most important meal. And it's important for you to be as good a model as possible for your kids in this area as well as in other aspects of your life. People who skip breakfast are more likely to eat between meals and often end up with more calories for the day than breakfast eaters. If your child sees that you eat a well-balanced breakfast, then maybe s/he will develop good eating habits, too.

Part of the problem stems from our breakfast food stereotype ideas as just illustrated. Maybe now is the time to change our habits of mealtime menus. A peanut butter sandwich, a hunk of cheese and whole wheat toast, or a container of yogurt are perfectly acceptable breakfast foods.

Leftovers have traditionally been the domain of lunch and dinner. Just for variation, why not serve leftover pizza, hamburger, casseroles, chops, spaghetti, etc. as breakfast? And have your eggs, cereal or something "breakfasty" for the noon or evening meal. And in a lot of cases, you don't even have to warm up the leftovers!

In case you have leftover spaghetti sauce, here's a good way to use it up:

PIZZA FOR BREAKFAST

> leftover spaghetti sauce
> English muffins
> cheese (Mozzarella, Cheddar, American, Colby, etc.)
> butter or margarine

Split your muffins and toast lightly, spread a little butter or margarine on and then top with a tablespoon or two of spaghetti sauce. (Optional additions can include bacon bits, mushrooms, etc.) Then lay a couple of slices of cheese on the top;

place your muffin pizza under the broiler and heat till the cheese is gooey (3-5 minutes).

Other non-traditional possibilities for breakfasts are:

- Grilled (or ungrilled) cheese sandwiches
- Cottage cheese
- Soup and cheese
- Eggnog drinks (see page 16)

The following recipes are aimed, to a great extent, towards making breakfast enjoyable and nutritious not only for your kids, but for your entire family.

EGGS

Eggs are a traditional part of the breakfast scene; some kids really go for them and others don't. Eggs are also good dinner fare. Here are a few ideas for interesting ways to prepare eggs that may not convert the egg-haters, but that might lure the "not-so-crazy-about-eggs" bunch!

BULL'S EYE

1 egg
1 slice bread
margarine or butter

Use a 2" round cookie cutter and cut out the center of the bread. Spread margarine generously on each side of the bread. Brown one side of the bread only in a moderately hot, greased frying pan and then turn over. Crack the egg into the hole in the bread and cook till the white is set. You may need to cover the pan to help the egg white set quickly. Lift out carefully and serve.

For the holidays, you may wish to use a heart-shaped cutter for Valentine's Day, a bunny for Easter, a bell at Christmas, etc.

BREAD OMELET

2 Tbsp. bread crumbs
2 Tbsp. milk
1 egg, separated
1/2 tsp. butter or margarine

Mix the bread crumbs and milk and let soak for
15 minutes, or you can do this the night before in
a covered bowl in the refrigerator. In another bowl,
beat the yolk well and also in a separate bowl beat
the egg white till stiff but not dry. Add the egg yolk
to the bread crumb mixture and then fold in the
beaten egg white. Cook in a small to medium-sized,
greased frying pan till it is set on the top and
browned on the bottom. Remove and serve with
butter, jelly or honey. Optional additions are bacon
bits, pieces of leftover meats, etc.

If you double this recipe, use a large frying pan
for cooking.

CONFETTI OMELET

1 egg, separated
1 Tbsp. milk
1/4 cup cottage cheese or grated Cheddar cheese
1 Tbsp. minced pimento
2 tsp. dried parsley
1 tsp. butter or margarine

Beat the egg yolk well. Add milk, cheese, pimento
and seasonings. Beat the egg white till stiff and fold
into yolk mixture. Heat shortening in a small to
medium-sized frying pan and add the egg mixture.
Cook over a low heat till set. DO NOT COVER.
Optional additions are bits of bacon, artificial bacon
bits, meats, herbs, etc.

EGG POSIES

If you happen to have a special tool for slicing hard-boiled eggs into uniform rounds, probably your 3 year old can perform this job for you. If you don't have this gadget, slice the eggs the short way with a serrated knife into ¼" thick slices.

    1 hard-boiled egg
    1 piece toasted and buttered bread
    jelly

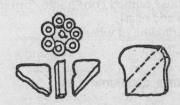

Slice the egg and arrange towards the top of a medium-sized plate so that they overlap and form a flower. Add a dab of jelly in the center of the flower. To make the leaves and stem, cut the slice of buttered toast into two triangles and one long strip and arrange as shown. Voila!

A tip on making hard-boiled eggs:
  If you have trouble with eggs cracking and the white coming out while cooking, try this method:

1) Place eggs in a deep kettle.
2) Add cold water to 1" higher than the tops of the eggs.
3) Heat until simmering (190°).
4) Cover pan, remove from the burner and let set for 20-25 minutes (depending on egg size) in this water.
5) Run cold water over eggs as usual, and peel.

SCRAMBLED EGGS (or Humpty Dumpty's Reprieve)

Scrambled eggs are generally acceptable to a large
portion of the under-five generation. Here are
a few suggestions to add a little spice and variety
to this old favorite:

   1) Sautéed onion, celery and/or green pepper;
   2) Crisp bacon bits, artificial bacon bits, leftover
      meats or cooked vegetables;
   3) Seasoned salad croutons;
   4) Cottage cheese or any grated cheese;
   5) Drained canned corn (sauté corn in fat and
      then add eggs);
   6) A sprinkling of wheat germ.

PEANUT BUTTER CUSTARD

   1⅓ cups milk
   ⅓ cup powdered milk
   ⅓ cup peanut butter
   2 eggs, beaten
   3 Tbsp. honey

Warm up the liquid milk; stir in powdered milk and
blend with peanut butter until smooth. Mix in the
eggs and honey and pour into greased custard cups.
Set the cups in a pan of hot water (water should
come up to the same level as the custard) and bake
30 minutes at 325° or until a knife inserted in the
center comes out clean. Refrigerate and serve cold.

BREAKFAST FRUIT COMBINATIONS

Vitamin C is a good part of breakfast, but again it
need not always be the traditional orange juice.
Consider some of these combinations:

1) Orange slices cut as circles;
2) Sliced peaches and blueberries;
3) Strawberries and pineapple chunks;
4) Apricots and cottage cheese;
5) Grapes, apples, etc. with cheese chunks;
6) Mandarin oranges with sour cream or yogurt;
7) Cantaloupe slices.

When serving an orange, roll it on the counter prior to cutting to get more juice.

Orange juice freshly squeezed is best but frozen is cheaper. Make sure it says "juice" and not drink and also no sugar added. Bottled Tropicana orange juice is good for baby's bottle as it is pure orange juice but has no pulp to stick in the nipple.

FROM THE GRIDDLE

Pancakes and waffles are lots of fun for the whole family and there are prepared mixes for both, plus frozen waffles which are real time savers. However, if you do have the time, here are some basic recipes that just could become a traditional part of your weekend breakfasts.

GREAT GROOVY GRIDDLE CAKES

1½ cups flour (white, whole wheat, or a
    combination)
1¾ tsp. baking powder
3 Tbsp. sugar or honey
2 eggs
3 Tbsp. melted shortening, or vegetable oil
1 or 1¼ cups milk

(continued on next page)

Combine dry ingredients in a large bowl. Beat eggs, add sugar and shortening and milk. Add wet ingredients to the dry and mix till barely moistened. Ignore the lumps. Let it set covered in a cool place as long as possible. Even make the batter the night before, if possible. Bake on a lightly greased griddle or frying pan. When bubbles appear on upper surface of the cakes, turn and brown second side.

BUTTERMILK BEAUTIES

> 1 cup flour (white, whole wheat or combination)
> 1 tsp. baking powder
> 1/2 tsp. soda
> 1 Tbsp. melted shortening or oil
> 1 egg
> 1 cup buttermilk (or plain yogurt or sweet milk or
>   water to make 1 cup of liquid)

Mix dry ingredients. Add milk and shortening to egg and mix. Combine the two mixtures until they are just moistened. Bake on a hot griddle, browning both sides.

COTTAGE CHEESE PANCAKES

> 3 eggs
> 1 cup cottage cheese
> 2 Tbsp. melted butter or salad oil
> 2 Tbsp. flour or cornmeal

With a small mixer (or in a blender) beat eggs; add cottage cheese and mix till fairly smooth. Add shortening and flour. Make cakes on the "smallish" side. Bake as usual for pancakes.

PERSONALIZED PANCAKES

For the child who is starting to learn letters and numbers, what fun it is to have a stack of pancakes with initials or age on the top of the cake on birthday morning, or maybe just a newly learned letter or number. Here's how you do it!

1) Dip a teaspoon into your pancake batter and let excess drip off.
2) Using the batter left on the tip of the spoon draw the letter or number *backwards* on the hot greased pan or griddle.

(You might need to practice your mirror-writing on paper.)

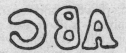

3) When the underside is lightly browned, pour a spoonful of regular batter *over* the letter or numbers so that the pancake will completely surround it.
4) Bake until bubbles appear; then turn and brown second side.

The letter or number will stand out darker than the surrounding pancake.

or maybe try **Animal Pancakes**, like so:

CRUMPETS

"Crumpets and tea" is an expression that crops up fairly regularly in English novels and films. Most Americans never have had crumpets. Now you can save your child from living in ignorance of this fine English tradition. This recipe is one of many different varieties.

    3 cups flour (white or half white and half whole wheat)
    1 Tbsp. baking powder
    2 Tbsp. sugar or honey
    2 Tbsp. butter or margarine
    1 egg
    1½ to 1¾ cups milk

Mix flour, baking powder, and sugar. Cut in shortening till mixture is like bread crumbs. Beat egg with 1½ cups milk. Combine wet and dry ingredients and stir just enough to moisten. (The batter should be thick, but if it doesn't spread when dropped on griddle, add some more milk.) Drop batter by tablespoons onto hot, greased griddle. Bake as usual for pancakes.

With any leftover batter, thin it with a bit more milk — make some larger cakes — and use instead of bread for a sandwich.

WONDERFUL WAFFLES

    2 cups flour (white or half white and half whole wheat)
    2 tsp. baking powder
    2 Tbsp. sugar or honey
    2 eggs, separated
    2 cups milk
    4-6 Tbsp. melted shortening or oil

Sift dry ingredients twice. (If using whole wheat flour, add particles back that would not go through.) Beat egg yolks, then mix with shortening (and honey, if using) and milk. Mix dry and liquid ingredients enough to just blend them. Beat egg whites till stiff and fold into batter. Bake according to manufacturer's instructions for your waffle iron.

Use leftover batter to make additional waffles and freeze them for later use. All you need to do is pop them in a toaster prior to eating. Or if you're super organized, make the whole batch ahead and freeze them for a series of yummy, fast breakfasts.

VARIATIONS ON THE PANCAKE AND WAFFLE THEME

- Fresh or frozen drained berries and a little extra sweetening. (If possible let batter sit ½ hour when adding fresh berries.)
- Chopped nut meats (again, let sit ¹/₂ hour if possible).
- Chopped raisins and nuts.
- Grated orange rind.
- Finely diced ham, bacon bits, etc.
- Add powdered milk.
- For waffles — pour batter and then place a piece of **uncooked** bacon on batter in each section of the iron. Close iron and bake as usual.
- Replace part of the flour called for with soy flour, wheat germ, brewer's yeast, or corn meal for more nutritional value.
- Divide batter and add a few drops of food coloring to each so you can offer a "colored" collection on a platter.

(continued on next page)

Suggested **toppings** for pancakes and waffles:

- Cinnamon and sugar/honey mixed.
- Peanut butter and jelly/honey.
- Ice cream topped with wheat germ.
- Sweetened apple sauce mixed with sour cream or yogurt.
- Canned or fresh fruits such as peaches, berries or bananas (roll pancakes around any of the above fruits, secure with a toothpick, and serve the "logs" with syrup and butter).
- Maple syrup or honey and butter — traditional.

(To make your own "maple" syrup, see page 101.)

FRENCH TOAST

French Toast is a good way to combine eggs, milk and bread. If you are going to use home-made whole-grain bread for this purpose, be very careful as you lift the slices from the egg-milk mixture into the pan, for they are usually more fragile than white bread after being soaked and can break easily.

Here are two batter recipes:

1 egg
1/3 cup milk
1/8 tsp. vanilla
(approx. 3 slices of bread)
or
1 egg
4 tsp. flour
1/3 cup milk (approx. 3 slices of bread)

For both recipes, beat eggs lightly and add next two ingredients. Dip bread into the mixture. Fry in a well greased pan over a fairly high heat, browning well on both sides. Or on a cold morning, preheat the oven to 500° and bake the dipped bread on a greased pan, turning after the top browns.

Serve with any of the suggested toppings for pancakes and waffles.

FRENCH TOAST WAFFLES

1 egg, beaten
1/4 cup milk
2 Tbsp. melted shortening or salad oil
Optional: 1-2 Tbsp. sugar or honey
1/2 tsp. cinnamon
bread slices

Combine all ingredients except the bread and mix well. Cut the bread to fit the waffle iron. Dip bread into the batter and bake on a hot, greased iron until well browned. (It may be necessary to hold the top of the iron down for a little while since the bread has more height than batter alone.)

FRENCH PANCAKES

1 slice of bread (preferably whole wheat)
1 egg
1/4 tsp. vanilla or maple extract
1 Tbsp. milk

Combine the above ingredients in a blender. Whir till smooth. Cook as for pancakes.

CEREALS

Cereals are one of the first foods we give our
children as infants, and they generally continue in
the diet as a breakfast staple. Historically cereals
began as a nourishing whole grain breakfast food.
But processing has changed the food value, though
not the tradition. There has been a lot published
about the lack of nutritional value in the highly
processed dry cereals on the market. Although, as
the cereal manufacturers state, a child does get
some vitamins and minerals, most of the nutritional
value comes from the accompanying serving of
milk. Some manufacturers have sprayed their cereals
with additional vitamins, giving you virtual vitamin
pellets which are not a good substitute for a whole-
grain or unprocessed cereal. In fact, according to
the Center for Science in the Public Interest in
Washington, D.C., Wheaties and Total are identical
in content. However, Total has ½ cent worth of
vitamins added per 12-oz. box but the price cost to
you is over 30 cents. Read your cereal labels!
Also, you will find that many of today's popular
cereals are mainly sugar . . . a poor way to start off
your day. It is cheaper and more nutritional for you
to add a teaspoonful of sugar or the equivalent
artificial sweetener to a non-sweetened cereal. It
"pays" to avoid those cereals that are sugar-frosted,
honey-coated or chocolate-flavored.

Some cereals that contain NO sugar are: Cream of
Wheat (farina), Quaker Oats, Kretschmer Wheat
Germ, and Wheatena. Add to that, Triscuits, even
though in cracker form, as a form of shredded
wheat. (Put it in a blender for your little ones.)

The sugar in many of the dry cereals tends to
encourage children to expect sweets along with the
main part of breakfast, as well as other meals.

But assuming that you are using a sweetener, consider that those below are listed in descending order of nutritional value*:

> Blackstrap molasses
> Brown sugar
> Maple sugar
> Honey (strained or extracted)
> White sugar

HOT CEREAL

There are quite a few kinds of hot cooked cereals on the market such as Malt-O-Meal, Roman Meal, Cream of Wheat and Rice, Oatmeal (Old-Fashioned variety), etc. These can be "pepped up" to look and taste better in any of the following ways:

- Mixing in raisins, dates, drained canned fruit, frozen fruit, and especially fresh fruit.
- Using any of the above to create a design on the bowl of cereal, such as a face with raisins for eyes and nose, and peach slices for mouth and ears; or a spiral design of jelly; a lacy design à la Jackson Pollack made by drizzling some molasses from a spoon. Use your imagination!
- Adding wheat germ, cooked soy grits, and/or powdered milk.
- One or two chocolate chips add a bit of adventure when hidden in a bowl of cereal.
- A heaping spoonful of creamy peanut butter.

---

* This is based on "Composition of Foods" by the U.S. Department of Agriculture.

HOMEMADE HOT RICE CEREAL

Grind several cups of raw brown rice to a fine
powder in a blender. Store it in a tightly covered
container.

 1/2 cup rice powder (as made above)
 2 cups milk
 dash of salt

In a small saucepan, bring milk and salt just to
the boiling point. Add the rice powder and stir
constantly. Lower heat, cover pan and simmer for
8-10 minutes. Serve with butter or margarine, honey,
molasses, wheat germ, fruit, etc. It has a nutty
taste.

CORN-OFF-THE-COB HOT CEREAL

 1/4 cup yellow corn meal
 1/4 cup cold water
 Optional: 2 tsp. wheat germ
 3/4 cup boiling water
 Optional: 1/4 cup powdered milk

Mix together corn meal, cold water and wheat germ,
if using. Bring the 3/4 cup water to a boil and add
the corn meal mixture and the powdered milk, if
using. Stirring constantly, bring to a boil and let boil
about two minutes. When it has cooled down to an
edible temperature, serve with any of the following:

 Butter or maragine
 Cottage cheese
 Sour cream or yogurt
 Jam, honey, brown sugar, maple syrup, raisins
    or chopped dates

COLD CEREAL

One idea for a nutritious and easy bowl of cereal is to take a whole-grain muffin and crumble it in a bowl. Pour milk over it, add fruit, nuts or sweetener and you have an instant breakfast.

The other rage of the cold cereal shelves these days is granola, which is being marketed under a variety of names. Check the list of ingredients carefully, as some have a high sugar content. But better yet, try making your own. It's easy, cheaper and the proportions of ingredients can be changed around to fit your family's preference. It can also be ground in a blender and served with milk to babies and young children who would choke on the unground cereal. Another way to soften granola is to let it sit in milk in a bowl overnight in the refrigerator.

GRANOLA

4 cups uncooked oatmeal
1 1/2 cups wheat germ (raw or toasted)
1 cup grated coconut
1/4 cup powdered milk
1-2 Tbsp. cinnamon
1 Tbsp. brown sugar
1/3 cup vegetable oil
1/2 cup honey
1 Tbsp. vanilla
Optionals:
1/2 cup sesame seeds
1/2 cup raw nuts, seeds or raisins, etc.

In a large bowl, mix dry ingredients. In a saucepan combine oil, honey and vanilla and warm. Add these to the dry ingredients and stir till all the particles are coated. (Hand mixing works well here.)

(continued on next page)

Spread this mixture out in a long, low pan or
rimmed baking sheets that have been greased, and
bake at either:

> 250° for an hour **or**
> 300° for half an hour

depending on your time schedule. Turn this with a
spatula from time to time. When finished toasting,
add your dried fruits such as raisins. When cool,
store in an airtight container.

WHEAT GERM

Raw wheat germ has greater nutritional value than
the toasted kind, but is less palatable. So it is
probably preferable to use it toasted as a breakfast
cereal and be assured your kids will like it. There
are several brands on the market, some with
additions such as honey, cinnamon, raisins, etc.
Serve any of these as regular cereal with milk
without making a big to-do about it and see what
reaction your kids have. Or, if you use raw wheat
germ in your cooking, and want to toast your
own, here's one way to do it.

> 4 cups raw wheat germ (always keep in refrigerator)
> 1/2 cup honey, approx. (warmed a bit)

Mix thoroughly and spread mixture on a well
greased baking sheet and baked at 300° for 10
minutes in bottom third of oven. Cool and put in
airtight container and keep refrigerated.

Additional serving ideas:

- Sprinkle on peanut butter sandwiches.
- Mix with other sandwich fillings.
- Add to meat loaf (approx. 1/4 cup).
- Toss a little in a green salad.

RICE PUDDING

Usually a hearty dessert, rice pudding is a nice change of pace for breakfast and includes milk, egg, and a grain.

> 2 cups cooked rice (preferably brown rice)
> 2 cups milk
> 1/2 cup powdered milk
> 1/4 cup brown sugar
> 1 Tbsp. butter or margarine, melted
> 2 eggs, well beaten
> 1/2 lemon rind, grated
> 1/2 tsp. vanilla
> 1/4 cup raisins
> bread crumbs or wheat germ

Mix all ingredients together except crumbs or wheat germ. Grease a 1-quart casserole dish (or individual custard cups) and sprinkle with some crumbs or wheat germ on the bottom. Pour in pudding mixture and sprinkle more crumbs on top. Bake at 350° for 20 minutes or until a knife inserted in the center comes out clean.

(For children, this is best prepared in advance and served cold.)

BREAKFAST COOKIES

Although you may not want to make a regular practice of it, nutritious cookies can be a fun and interesting breakfast, as well as good for snacks and desserts.

BACON 'N EGG COOKIES

1¼ cups flour (white or whole wheat)
⅔ cup brown sugar
½ cup Grape Nuts cereal
½ lb. bacon, cooked crisp & crumbled **or**
½ cup artificial bacon bits
½ cup shortening, melted
1 egg, beaten
2 Tbsp. frozen orange juice concentrate, undiluted
1 Tbsp. grated orange peel

Mix flour, sugar, Grape Nuts and bacon. Add remaining ingredients and blend well. Drop by tablespoonfuls onto a sheet (ungreased if real bacon is used, otherwise, grease the cookie sheet) and bake at 350° for 10-12 minutes or until cookies are a light brown.

BANANA OATMEAL COOKIES

¾ cup shortening
1 cup brown sugar
1 egg, beaten
1½ cups flour (white, whole wheat, or a
    combination)
½ tsp. soda
1 tsp. cinnamon
¼ tsp. nutmeg
1 cup mashed banana
1¾ cups oatmeal, uncooked

Cream shortening with sugar and then add the egg and mix well. Mix flour, soda, cinnamon and nutmeg together and add to creamed mixture and blend till smooth. Add mashed banana and oatmeal next. Blend. Drop by teaspoonfuls onto a greased sheet and bake at 400° for 12-15 minutes.

Optional additions: raisins, nuts, wheat germ, sunflower seeds, grated orange peel, etc.

OATMEAL OVERNIGHT COOKIES

In the evening, combine:
4 cups oatmeal, uncooked
2 cups brown sugar
1 cup bland oil

The next morning add:

2 eggs, beaten
1 tsp. flavoring (vanilla or almond)
Option: 1/4 cup wheat germ

Mix well. Drop by spoonfuls onto a greased cookie sheet and bake at 300° for 12-15 minutes. Watch them carefully. Remove cookies from sheet while still warm or you may never get them off later.

HINT: Many cookie recipes can be thinned with a little milk and baked in a square pan for bars so that you will have two versions of the same recipe.

GRANOLA COOKIES

1 cup butter or margarine
1 1/2 cups brown sugar, packed
    (or 1/2 brown-1/2 white)
2 eggs, beaten well
1 1/2 tsp. vanilla
1 cup raisins or 1 (6 oz.) pkg. chocolate chips
1 1/2 cups flour (white, whole wheat or a
    combination)
1 tsp. baking soda
1 cup oatmeal, uncooked
2 cups granola
Optional: 1/2 cup chopped walnuts

Cream shortening till smooth. Add sugar and blend. Add remaining ingredients and mix well. Drop mixture onto a greased cookie sheet and bake at 350° until lightly browned on bottom, 10-12 minutes.

GRANOLA BREAKFAST BARS

   2 cups granola
   2 eggs, beaten
   Optional: Dash of vanilla for sweetening

Combine the granola and eggs in a greased 8"
square pan. Bake at 350° for 15 minutes. Cut into
8 bars. When serving spread with jam, honey or
peanut butter.

WHEELS OF STEEL

   ½ cup butter or margarine
   ½ cup peanut butter
   1 cup brown sugar, packed
   1 egg, beaten
   1 tsp. vanilla
   ¾ cup whole wheat flour
   1 cup oatmeal, uncooked
   ¼ cup wheat germ, raw or toasted
   ½ cup powdered milk
   ¼ tsp. baking powder and soda each
   3 Tbsp. liquid milk
   1 cup raisins
   Optional: sesame seeds

Cream shortening till smooth. Add peanut butter,
sugar, egg, and vanilla and beat well. In a separate
bowl combine flour, wheat germ, dry milk, baking
powder and soda. Add the dry ingredients to the wet
and stir well. Add liquid milk, oats and raisins. Blend.
On a greased cookie sheet place a heaping spoonful
of dough and spread it into a circle. Leave an inch
or more between cookies as they spread. Sprinkle
with sesame seeds on top and press into dough.
Bake at 375° for 10-12 minutes. Allow cookies to
cool before removing as they are very fragile while
warm.

CEREAL BALLS

> **1** cup ground-in-a-blender cereal (shredded wheat,
>   granola, wheat germ, etc.)
> **1** Tbsp. honey
> milk — as much as needed
> Optional: 1 Tbsp. peanut butter

After grinding cereal, add honey, peanut butter,
and blend. Add as much milk as necessary so that
mixture can be rolled into balls. Refrigerate in a
covered container.

Additional variations:

- Roll into logs and roll these in coconut or
  wheat germ.
- When traveling, add powdered milk and
  brown sugar (eliminating the peanut butter)
  instead of the liquid milk and the honey, and
  store in a plastic bag. When needed, just
  add water for preparation as a breakfast food
  or snack.

CREAMY BALLS

Combine chopped nuts and cream cheese. Roll
into balls and serve.

QUICK BREADS AND MUFFINS

If you already have some quick bread recipes in
your repertoire that are popular with your family,
you could substitute whole wheat flour for part of
the white flour called for. Or use the Cornell
Triple-Rich Flour Formula (see page 75) with the
flour you're using. If, however, you are substituting
whole-grain flour for white, be sure to increase the
baking powder called for, as whole grains require
a bit more help in rising.

PEANUT BUTTER BREAD

This slices best if baked a day in advance and
refrigerated after cooking.

    2 cups flour (white, whole wheat or a combination)
    4 tsp. baking powder
    1/4 cup sugar or honey
    1 1/4 cups milk
    2/3 cup peanut butter

Lightly mix dry ingredients together in a large bowl.
If using honey, cream it with the peanut butter in
a separate bowl. Heat the milk till lukewarm, then
add the peanut butter and blend well. Add the
wet and dry ingredients and beat thoroughly. Pour
into a greased loaf pan and bake at 350° for 45-50
minutes. When the bread is cold, make thin slices
and spread with honey or jam.

BREAKFAST BANANA NUT BREAD

    1/4 cup butter or margarine
    1/2 cup brown sugar
    1 egg, beaten
    1 cup bran cereal or uncooked oatmeal
    4-5 mashed ripe bananas (about 1 1/2 cups)
    1 tsp. vanilla
    1 1/2 cups flour (white, whole wheat or a
        combination)
    2 tsp. baking powder
    1/2 tsp. baking soda
    1/2 cup chopped nuts

Cream shortening and sugar until light. Add egg
and mix well. Then add the cereal, bananas and
vanilla. Stir. Combine the remaining ingredients
in a bowl and add to the first mixture, stirring only
long enough to moisten the flour. Grease or oil
a loaf pan, and then flour; pour in batter. Bake at
350° for an hour or until bread tests as done.

HINT: What to do with that leftover, ripe banana? Mash it, add a bit of lemon juice or Fruit Fresh, and freeze till you plan to make some more banana bread.

If chopped nuts aren't yet appropriate for your child, whirl them in a blender before adding to batter.

READY BRAN MUFFINS

The proportions called for in this recipe make several quart jars full of batter. If it's too much, either cut the recipe in half or give some to a neighbor, unless you have extra room in the freezer.

POUR	2 cups boiling water over 2 cups 100% bran cereal
CREAM	1 cup shortening (butter, Crisco, margarine, etc.) with 2 cups sugar or 1⅔ cups honey
ADD	4 eggs, beaten 1 quart buttermilk
ADD	the above bran mixture and mix.

Fold in the dry ingredients, which are as follows:

　5 cups flour (white or a combination of whole wheat
　　　& white)
　5 tsp. soda
　4 cups 100% bran cereal

Store in jars in the refrigerator for as long as six weeks.

To bake, preheat oven to 375°, fill greased muffin tins ¾ full and bake 20-25 minutes.

Optional additions to some or all of the muffins: blueberries, chopped fresh apples, raisins, chopped dates, coconut, nuts, peanuts, a cube of cheese, etc.

For a change, fill a loaf pan half full and bake at 350° until done.

WHOLE WHEAT MUFFINS

1 cup whole wheat flour
¾ cup white flour
¼ cup sugar or honey
4 tsp. baking powder
1 egg
1 cup milk
¼ cup salad oil

Mix dry ingredients. In a separate small bowl, beat egg slightly and stir in milk and oil. Add wet ingredients to the dry and stir till just moistened. Batter will be lumpy. Bake in greased muffin tins ⅔ full for 20-25 minutes at 400°. Remove muffins from tins immediately after baking.

ORANGE MUFFINS

1 slice bread (whole grain preferred)
1 egg
⅓ cup powdered milk
½ tsp. baking soda
1 orange, peeled and cut up
1 Tbsp. water
4 tsp. honey or sugar

Pull apart the bread with a fork in a bowl. Mix the rest of the ingredients together and combine with the bread. Spoon into greased muffin cups, ⅔ full, and bake at 350° for 30 minutes.

OATMEAL MUFFINS

1 cup oatmeal, uncooked
½ tsp. soda
1 cup flour
1 tsp. baking powder
1 tsp. vinegar plus milk to equal 1 cup of liquid (let
    stand 5 min.)

1 egg, beaten
⅓ cup brown sugar
⅓ cup salad oil

Combine the oatmeal, soda; add flour and baking powder. In another bowl, mix the remaining ingredients. Then stir the wet ingredients with the dry till just moistened. Fill greased muffin cups ⅔ full and bake at 400° for 15-20 minutes.

QUICKIE TURNOVERS

1 (8 oz.) can refrigerated crescent rolls
Filling:
  ½ cup honey
  1 Tbsp. sunflower seeds
  1 Tbsp. raisins
  ¼ cup blueberries

Combine all the ingredients listed for the filling. Unroll the crescent rolls and place a spoonful of the filling mixture in the middle of each triangle of dough. Moisten the edges of the dough and fold point A over to point C on the diagram and press edges firmly together.

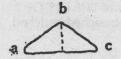

Place on a greased cookie sheet and bake at 375° for 10-12 minutes.

Other filling suggestions:

Peanut Butter	Jelly or honey
Jelly	Granola
Powdered Milk *or*	Apple slices
Raisins	Cinnamon & nuts

BREAD

If baking bread just isn't "your thing," consider
using the frozen dough breads in your grocer's
freezer section. You let them thaw and rise, then
bake. Most don't contain all those extra ingredients
to make bread shelf-stable. The major disadvantage
of frozen dough bread is that because it is difficult
to slice thin, and because it tastes and smells so
good . . . it disappears very quickly.

The art of bread-making is starting to come back
into its own in this country. If you've never tried
it, why not start now? Being home with small
children gives you the type of time slots needed
for making bread, that is, 5 to 10 minutes of
concentrated work spread over several hours.

The aroma of yeast bread baking is a real delight,
one to which you and your family could take a real
liking.

You have probably noticed in this book that when
flour is called for the recipe generally gives you
a choice of white, whole wheat, or a mixture of the
two. Here is what the authors of THE JOY OF
COOKING have to say about bleached enriched
white flour:

> "After the removal of the outer coats and germ,
> our flours may be enriched, but the term is
> misleading. Enriched flours contain only four of
> the many ingredients known to have been
> removed from it in the milling."

Nonetheless, you can give additional food value to
white flour for cakes, cookies, muffins, breads, etc.,
by this simple method:

Cornell Triple Rich Flour Formula

Before putting any flour into the measuring cup, place in the bottom of your one cup measure:

1 Tbsp. soy flour
1 Tbsp. dry milk
1 tsp. wheat germ

Then add flour to make one cup. Do this for each cup of flour used. Eventually you may want to try adding a little more of each of the enrichers. Whole-grain flours, too, benefit from this formula.

Bread-Making Procedures

In case you're wondering about how to tell if the dough or batter has **doubled in bulk,** here's an easy way to find out. Press lightly with one or two fingers near the edge of the bread. If a small indentation remains, it has doubled. If not doubled, the dough will spring back.

To tell **when bread is done,** remove it from the pan and tap on the bottom. If there is a hollow sound, it is done. If it goes "thud" you'd better put it back another 5-10 minutes.

If the bread is **browning too fast** (i.e., it's already a light brown after only 10-15 minutes) cover the top lightly with a piece of aluminum foil.

If you've **never kneaded,** don't let that stop you. It's a procedure that improves with practice so start experimenting now. It is a process of folding the dough and pressing down with the heel of your hand, over and over again, until the dough becomes smooth, elastic, and is no longer sticky. You may need to sprinkle flour on the dough and/or your working surface when you first begin until the dough loses some of its "stickiness."

SAY, MOM . . . **if there's no warm place to let your bread rise** where busy little fingers can't reach, try placing a baking pan filled with about an inch of hot water on the bottom of your oven. Put the bowl or pans of dough that are rising on the middle shelf. You will have to look at the pan of water every half hour or so to see if it needs to be "hotted up." And don't forget to remove the pan of water when you bake your bread!

Or turn oven on at 200° for 60 seconds. Turn off. Then put bread in for rising.

BASIC WHOLE WHEAT BREAD

1 cup warm water (105-115°)
2 pkgs. yeast
1 Tbsp. honey
2 cups milk
1/4 cup butter, margarine, or oil
1/3 cup honey
1 1/2 Tbsp. salt
5 cups whole wheat flour
3 cups white flour
Optional: 1/4 cup wheat germ

1. Dissolve 2 pkgs. of yeast in one cup warm water. Stir in 1 Tbsp. honey. Let sit 10 minutes.
2. In a saucepan combine 2 cups milk, 1/4 cup butter or margarine or oil, 1/3 cup honey and 1 1/2 Tbsp. salt. Heat till lukewarm. Do not scald.
3. Pour warm milk mixture and dissolved yeast into a large mixing bowl.
4. Add the whole wheat flour, one cup at a time, beating well after each addition. Be sure to

get all the whole wheat flour in. Add enough white flour to make a soft yet manageable dough.

5. Turn out on a lightly floured board and knead until smooth and elastic, 8-10 minutes.
6. Place in a greased bowl, turning dough to grease the top.
7. Cover and let rise in a warm, draft-free place until doubled in bulk.
8. Punch down, divide in half and knead each half about 30 seconds.
9. Shape into loaves and place in three greased loaf pans.
10. Cover and let rise again until doubled in bulk, about ¾ hour.
11. Preheat oven to 400° and bake 40 minutes or till done.

CINNAMON SWIRL BREAD

Before shaping the dough, roll out to a rectangle that is about 6x16"; mix together 4 Tbsp. brown sugar and 4 Tbsp. cinnamon; sprinkle ¼ cup of this mixture over each rectangle, beginning with the narrow side, roll up tightly into a loaf; seal ends and bottom by pinching dough together to make a seam; place in the loaf pans and proceed as usual.

This next bread recipe is an especially good one for you if you have an outside job or are too busy during the day with the kids or whatever to make bread. Mix the dough in the evening, set it in the refrigerator and let it rise and bake the next evening.

REFRIGERATOR 100% WHOLE WHEAT BREAD

5 cups milk or water*
2 pkgs. dry yeast, dissolved in
     1 cup warm water (105-115°)
1/2 cup melted shortening or oil
1/4 cup molasses
1/4 cup honey
11-12 cups whole wheat flour
2 Tbsp. salt
Optional: 1-2 cups soy flour

1. In a 6-qt. pan or bowl, mix together the liquid, dissolved yeast, shortening, honey, molasses and salt.
2. Add flour gradually, mixing well after each addition. (If using soy flour, add after at least 4 cups of whole wheat has been added.) THIS DOUGH WILL BE MORE MOIST THAN ORDINARY BREAD DOUGH.
3. Let dough rest in the bowl 10-15 minutes.
4. Turn dough out on a floured board and knead for about 10 minutes, adding as little extra flour as possible.
5. Replace in the bowl, cover with foil or a dampened cloth and refrigerate immediately for 3 to 24 hours.
6. When ready to use, remove from the refrigerator, punch down and let stand 30 to 60 minutes at room temperature.
7. Divide into four equal portions, shape into loaves and place in four well greased loaf pans. Lightly grease the tops of the loaves.
8. Let rise in a warm, draft-free place until *almost* doubled in bulk.

---

* If the dough is to be refrigerated for only 3 hours, use luke-warm liquid; if it is to be left longer, cool liquid so dough will not rise too much. Dough may still require punching down a few times while it is in the refrigerator.

9. Preheat oven to 425°, place pans in the oven, reduce heat to 325° and bake for 1 hour or until done.

If your oven won't hold four pans at one time or you don't own four pans, remove only enough dough from the refrigerator as you can bake at one time. But be sure to take the rest out and use it within 24 hours.

This dough makes excellent hamburger buns. Use ¼ to ⅓ cup of dough for each bun. Bake at 325° for 25-30 minutes or till done.

TRIPLE RICH BATTER WHITE BREAD

Batter breads are somewhat simpler than breads that have to be kneaded. So this might be a good one for a new bread baker to start off with.

> 1 cup milk
> 3 Tbsp. sugar or honey
> 1 Tbsp. salt
> 2 Tbsp. melted shortening or vegetable oil
> 1 cup warm water (105-115°)
> 2 pkgs. dry yeast
> 4¼ cups unsifted white flour plus:
>
> soy flour ⎫ *See Cornell Triple Rich*
> dry milk ⎬ *Formula on page 75*
> wheat germ ⎭

1. Scald milk; stir in sugar (honey), salt, and shortening. Let cool to lukewarm (105-115°).
2. Add yeast to the warm water in a large bowl and stir till dissolved.
3. Pour warm milk mixture into the yeast.
4. Stir in the flour, 1 cup at a time, placing the soy flour, dry milk and wheat germ in the bottom of the measuring cup first.

(continued on next page)

5. Beat for about two minutes with a long-handled spoon.
6. Cover with a cloth and let rise in a warm, draft-free place until more than doubled in bulk, about 40 minutes.
7. Stir batter down and beat vigorously for about 30 seconds.
8. Grease two 9x5x3" loaf pans and divide batter evenly between them. Batter does not need to rise again.
9. Bake the loaves for about 50 minutes in a preheated 375° oven.

Variation: Try using part or all whole wheat flour. Beat a minute or two longer than for white flour in step 5.

Optional: Add one or more beaten eggs. You may prefer the texture.

BATTER RYE BREAD

> 1¼ cups warm water (105-115°)
> 1 pkg. dry yeast
> 2 tsp. honey
> 2 tsp. salt
> 2 Tbsp. melted shortening or vegetable oil
> 1 cup rye flour
> 1 cup whole wheat flour
> 1¾ cups white flour
> Optional: 1 Tbsp. caraway seed

1. Measure warm water into a large mixing bowl and add the yeast, honey and salt. Cover and let stand about 5 minutes until the yeast is dissolved.
2. Add shortening, optional caraway seed, rye flour and 1 cup white flour and beat vigorously with a long-handled spoon for about 2 minutes, OR blend on low speed of an electric mixer, scraping sides and bottom of bowl often.

3. Add remaining flours and stir with a spoon until smooth.
4. Cover and let rise in a warm, draft-free place until doubled in bulk, about 45-60 minutes.
5. Stir batter down, beating about 25 strokes.
6. Grease a loaf pan and place batter in, smoothing out the top with a floured hand.
7. Cover and let rise until dough reaches top of the pan, about 40 minutes.
8. Preheat oven to 375° and bake the single loaf 45-50 minutes or until done.

RAISIN 'N EGG BATTER BREAD

This bread has a rich cake-like quality.

> 1 cup milk
> 1/2 cup sugar or honey
> 1 tsp. salt
> 1/4 cup shortening or vegetable oil
> 1/2 cup warm water (105-115°)
> 2 pkgs. dry yeast
> 1 egg, beaten
> 4 1/2 cups white flour
> 1 cup raisins
> Optional: Cornell Triple Rich Formula

1. Scald milk; stir in sugar (honey), salt and shortening. Let cool to lukewarm (105-115°).
2. Add yeast to warm water in a large bowl and stir until dissolved.
3. Pour the warm milk mixture into the yeast.
4. Add the egg and then mix in three cups of the flour, beating well after each addition. After the third cup, beat till smooth.
5. Stir in remaining flour to make a stiff batter.
6. Cover with a cloth and let rise in a warm, draft-free place until doubled in bulk, about one hour.

(continued on next page)

7. Stir batter down and beat in raisins, distributing them as evenly as possible.
8. Grease two 1 qt. casserole dishes or two loaf pans and divide the batter evenly between them. Batter does not need to rise again.
9. Preheat oven to 350° and bake bread for 40-45 minutes or until done.

SWISS CHEESE BREAD

This bread tastes very nearly like a grilled Swiss cheese sandwich when toasted. And its braided, glazed top makes it very pretty!

1½ cups milk
2 Tbsp. sugar or honey
1 Tbsp. salt
2 Tbsp. butter, margarine or oil
2 cups grated Swiss cheese (8 oz.)
2 pkgs. dry yeast
½ cup warm water (105-115°)
5 cups white flour (approximately)
Optional: 1 egg and poppy or sesame seeds

1. Scald milk and combine with sugar (honey), salt, shortening and cheese in a large bowl. (Cheese will probably melt into a lump, but don't worry.) Let cool until lukewarm.
2. Dissolve yeast in the warm water and add to the cooled milk mixture. Stir well.
3. Gradually add flour, stirring well after each addition until a fairly stiff dough is formed.
4. Knead dough about 5-8 minutes.
5. Place in a greased bowl, turning to grease top; let it rise in a warm, draft-free place until doubled in bulk.
6. Punch down and divide the dough into 2 equal portions.

Pizza for Breakfast?   83

7. Roll each piece out into an 11x15" rectangle.
8. Cut each rectangle into 3 equal strips (the long way), leaving the strips joined at one end.

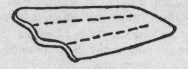

9. Braid the strips loosely. Pinch the 3 ends together.
10. Place each braided loaf in a well greased pan, cover and let rise until doubled.
11. Just before poppin' them in the oven, beat the egg with 1 Tbsp. cool water and brush onto tops of loaves. Sprinkle on seeds.
12. Bake 40-45 minutes in an oven preheated to 350°.

ENGLISH MUFFINS

A 7 oz. tuna-type can with both ends removed is a perfect cutter for the muffins. But for fun, try cutting them with large not too detailed cookie cutters. Some won't keep their shape and some will.

    1 cup milk, scalded
    2 Tbsp. sugar or honey
    1/4 cup butter, oil, or margarine
    1 Tbsp. salt
    Corn meal
    1 cup warm water (105-115°)
    1 pkg. dry yeast
    5-6 cups flour (white, whole wheat or a combination)

1. Place hot milk in a large bowl and add shortening, sugar (honey) and salt. Let cool to lukewarm.

(continued on next page)

2. Dissolve yeast in the warm water and add to the cooled milk.

3. Add 3 cups of flour and beat until smooth.

4. Gradually add more flour, beating well after each addition until a soft dough is formed.

5. Turn out on a lightly floured board and knead until smooth and elastic (8-10 minutes), adding more flour as necessary.

6. Place in a greased bowl, turning to grease the top; cover and let rise in a warm, draft-free place until doubled in bulk (about 1 hour).

7. Punch down and divide in half.

8. On a lightly floured board, roll the first half out to about ½ inch thick and cut as many circles of dough as you can.

9. Gently remove to a cookie sheet that has been heavily sprinkled with corn meal. Sprinkle tops with corn meal, too.

10. Push scraps together, roll out and cut again. Do this for the second half too, until all the dough is used.

11. Cover the muffins with a cloth and let rise until doubled.

12. To bake, heat a griddle or electric fry pan to moderately hot (about 300°) and grease lightly. Move muffins carefully with a large spatula to the griddle, fitting as many on without touching as you can. Bake until bottoms are browned (10-15 minutes) and then turn and bake other side.

This is a good summer bread because you don't have to turn on the oven.

To cut, insert tines of a fork all the way around and pull apart.

BAGELS

1½ cups warm water (105-115°)
1 pkg. dry yeast
1 Tbsp. salt
3 Tbsp. sugar or honey
4-6 cups flour (white, whole wheat or a combination)
1 egg
Optional: poppy or sesame seeds

1. In a large bowl, mix warm water with yeast and add salt and sugar (honey). Cover bowl and let stand 5 minutes.
2. Gradually add the flour until a soft to medium dough is obtained, but not a stiff dough.
3. Knead on a lightly floured board, 5-10 minutes until shiny and smooth, adding a little more flour as necessary for kneading.
4. Place in a greased bowl, turning to grease the top. Cover and let rise in a warm, draft-free place until doubled, about 30 minutes.
5. Punch down and knead lightly.
6. Shape into bagels by rolling approximately ¼ cup dough into a strand about 7 inches long and then pinching the ends firmly together. (You'll have about 12-15 bagels.)
7. Place the bagels fairly close together on a floured board or cookie sheet, cover and let rise again about 30 minutes in a warm place.
8. In the meantime, bring about 5 inches of water to a boil in a fairly large open kettle. Turn heat down so water is simmering.
9. When the bagels have risen, gently lift them one at a time and drop them into the simmering water. Turn them immediately and let simmer for about 2 minutes until puffy but not disintegrating. Several bagels may be in the water at one time, just so the pan is not too crowded.

(continued on next page)

10. Remove the bagels to a towel-covered area and let drain and cool while you are boiling the next batch.
11. Place the cooled bagels on a greased baking sheet. They can be quite close together.
12. Beat the egg briefly with 1 Tbsp. of cool water and brush over the tops of the bagels. Sprinkle with poppy or sesame seeds, if desired.
13. Bake for 30-40 minutes in an oven preheated to 375°.

This procedure may look complicated at first, but once you get the knack, you can turn out a batch in 3 to 3½ hours, from start to finish.

Summer Fall
Winter Spring

The following are a list of seasonal ideas that are often more fun than nutritious, but worth trying on occasion. There are a lot of "sugary" ideas here which should be served in moderation.

SUMMER

Summer means little hands constantly opening the refrigerator in search of "things" to quench thirst and hunger.

YOGURT POPSICLES

> 1 carton plain yogurt
> 1 (6 oz.) concentrated unsweetened fruit juice
>   (orange seems to be the favorite)
> Optional: dash of vanilla and/or honey

Mix well and freeze in molds. 3-oz. paper cups
work well as molds. For handles insert wooden sticks
or spoons when mixture is partially frozen.

Variation: Make "single servings" by mixing in a
small paper cup, some plain yogurt with pureed
canned or ripe fruit, or a spoonful of jam or jelly.
If too tart, add a bit of vanilla.

FUDGESICLES

> 1 (4 oz.) pkg. regular chocolate pudding mix (or
>   dietetic choc. mix)
> 3½ cups milk (skim)

Prepare as for pudding. Sweeten to taste. (An egg
may be added for additional nutritional value.)
Freeze in molds or paper cups and insert "handles."

QUICKIE POPS

In a mold or paper cup, mix juice (apple, pineapple,
orange, grapes, etc.) with 1 tsp. melted vanilla ice
cream. Mix well and put in freezer. Add handle
when partially frozen. This has the advantage of
being able to make just one or two rather than a
whole batch. Also a good way of helping down
some orange juice if you're meeting with resistance
when it's served in a glass, or just using up some
orange juice left from breakfast.

Variation: Mash pitted watermelon cubes (or blend)
and pour into a mold to make a popsicle.

BANANA POPS

Peel bananas, cut in half. Push wooden stick up
center of each half and freeze. Serve as such, or dip
in honey and roll in toasted wheat germ. If you
have the time and inclination, melt 6 oz. of
chocolate chip bits (or 12 oz. if you are using
6 bananas) plus a few tablespoons of water, then
dip the frozen banana into the chocolate and coat
to cover. Twirl to remove excess or avoid the
chocolate altogether and dip it in honey prior to
eating. (Optional: Roll in nuts or granola.) After the
chocolate sets, wrap in foil and store in the freezer.

To use up the leftover chocolate, add raisins, nuts,
coconut, wheat germ, etc. and drop by teaspoonful
on a sheet and cool in the refrigerator for some
nutritious candy.

DO-IT-YOURSELF ICE CREAM SANDWICHES

Spread softened ice cream to the edge of any
appropriate cookie (graham crackers are good, but
most any will do). Press on top cookie gently.
Wrap or stack in foil or plastic wrap and freeze.

ICES

Make a base syrup by cooking:

>   2 cups water
>   2 cups sugar

on a low boil for 10 minutes or till approximately
jelly stage on a candy thermometer.

Orange Ice — 2 cups fresh orange juice
              1/4 cup lemon juice or juice from 1 lemon

(continued on next page)

Grape Ice —   1½ cups grape juice
                ⅔ cup orange juice
                3 Tbsp. lemon juice
Lemon Ice —   ¾ cup lemon juice
                1 Tbsp. grated lemon peel
                2 cups water

Pour into trays or a small mixing bowl and put in
freezer. Watch for mushy stage (1 hour) then mix in
the tray and freeze. (Good alone or served by
the scoop in a fruit drink.)

Summer Drinks

All drinks seem to disappear from the refrigerator
extra fast at this time of year. Keeping a good supply
is no easy matter, so here are a few extra ideas:

APPLE JUICE — Try the frozen concentrate; it's
good, sugarless and can always be stretched a bit.
It can also be reconstituted with sparkling soda for
a change.

LEMONADE — Into a large container (pitcher or
bowl — 2 qts.), put three sliced lemons and 1 cup
of sugar. With a large spoon, pound the lemons to
release the juice. Stir. Add a batch of ice cubes
and let sit a while, then add water to fill and mix and
serve.

  Or try:

    1 cup of reconstituted lemon juice
    1½ cups sugar
    2 quarts of water

Mix and Serve.

GRAPE JUICE — You can double any amount of
grape juice from a bottle by adding an equal amount
of water and for each two cups of water added,
using ½ cup sugar and one to two fresh lemons.

This takes away the "heaviness" from pure grape juice and gives you more for your money.

FRUIT DRINK — To a glass of lemonade or light carbonated drink, add fresh fruit (pineapple, grapes, strawberries, etc.) and serve with a fork or toothpick plus a straw.

Water kept **cold** in the refrigerator is an excellent way of encouraging consumption of this inexpensive, sugar-free beverage.

Summer Picnics

Summer time means picnic time, whether you camp out or simply cook out. A backyard is as exciting to a child as a national campsite may be to Mom and Dad. And don't forget your front stoop for picnic lunch.

You can simplify any picnic by putting your meal on a skewer! Try a cube of cheese, ham (any meat) along with pineapple chunks, cherry tomatoes, pickles, etc. on a stick and bagged. Your meal can be eaten right off the stick or slid into a hot dog bun. The same will work for dessert . . . whether cookies and marshmallows for toasting or just a selection of fruits.

Finger JELL-O (see page 40) is a terrific picnic fare, assuming you're not going to the desert.

Don't overlook the magic of a marshmallow roast. Under 3 year olds will probably eat them uncooked off their stick* and still think it's a nifty event. If it's a backyard cookout, let your child later invite some of his neighborhood pals over for a social event of their own.

---

* BEWARE OF CHILDREN RUNNING AND EATING FROM STICKS AT THE SAME TIME!

S'MORES — The Traditional Recipe!

Place a toasted marshmallow and 4 squares of a
Hershey bar between two graham crackers, and
you've done it!

July 4th — Independence Day

This is the only major summer holiday, so add a
little red-white-blue to your table.

Make or buy cupcakes with white frosting and top
with several small red candles which will simulate
firecrackers when lit.

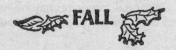 **FALL**

APPLE CIDER

In a saucepan — Heat apple cider, but do not boil.
Add a stick of cinnamon and a few cloves.

In a glass coffee percolator — Put whole spices,
such as stick cinnamon and cloves in the percolator
basket. Pour apple juice into the bottom container.
Let perk a few minutes until spiced to your taste.

HOT CHOCOLATE MIX

   1 (25 oz.) box powdered milk
   1 (1 lb.) box of instant cocoa
   1 (6 oz.) jar of CoffeeMate
   1 cup sugar

Mix well. Add 3 to 4 Tbsp. mix to 1 cup of boiling
water.

DONUTS

Use 1 pkg. refrigerated biscuit dough. Punch a hole
in the middle of each biscuit (a bottle cap will
work) and fry in 1" hot oil for about 1 minute or
until lightly brown on both sides. Fry the "holes,"
too. When cool, shake in a bag of: cinnamon and
sugar, or brown sugar or powdered sugar.

POPCORN

Any and all forms are loved. (Although not
recommended for children under 3 years.) It's as
much fun to make and watch as it is to eat.

TLC PEANUT BUTTER

If you've never made your own peanut butter, now
is the time to try a batch. It's a good rainy day . . .
or any day . . . activity. The challenge is not to
eat more than you shell.

1 lb. (or less) peanuts in the shell.

Shell and chop till fine in a blender one cup at
a time. Add 1-2 Tbsp. cooking oil. (Add salt only
if **not** salted in the shell.) This makes about 1 cup of
delicious peanut butter which should be stored in
the refrigerator.

You may also want to experiment with other kinds
of nuts, such as almonds, cashews, walnuts, etc.

You can take the easy way out and buy peanuts
already shelled.

EASY APPLESAUCE

Take advantage of the fall harvest for making some
fresh applesauce. Peel, core and slice several
apples. In a blender place ¼ cup water or apple
juice and add apples one at a time. Blend until
smooth. Pour into a saucepan and cook on low heat
5 to 10 minutes. Add cinnamon and sweetener
(honey or light corn syrup, etc.) to taste. A dash
of lemon or Fruit Fresh will retard its "darkening"
action.

SPELLIN' COOKIES

With school in progress, help with the homework by
making three letter cookie words. Using ⅓ cup of
water and 1 pkg. of gingerbread mix or a cuttin'
cookie recipe (see below) cut 3" round cookies.
Place them on a greased cookie sheet and with a
knife cut across the circle in thirds and push the
pieces slightly apart. Bake. When cool, make 3 letter
words with frosting . . . one letter on each piece.

CUTTIN' COOKIES

Combine: 3 eggs, beaten
          ½ cup corn oil
          1 cup sugar
          1 tsp. vanilla flavoring
          3 cups flour
          1 tsp. baking powder

Work on a well-floured surface. You may wish to
chill the dough before rolling out. Bake at 350
degrees for 8-10 minutes.

Or for a second variation combine:

½ cup shortening	1 tsp. milk
1 cup sugar	2 cups flour
1 egg	1 tsp. baking powder
1 Tbsp. milk	1 tsp. nutmeg

Roll out on a floured surface. Bake on a greased cookie sheet at 375 degrees for 6-8 minutes.

Consider using your Play-Dough shape makers for extra fun and games! Or use your child's hand as a shape to cut around.

EDIBLE DECORATING GLUE

Spread cookie with a thin coating of honey, then dip it into shredded coconut, toasted wheat germ or cookie decors.

 HALLOWEEN

Halloween is the holiday second only to Christmas for your child. Full understanding of Halloween comes at a surprisingly early age . . . costumes and candy, and not necessarily in that order.

Enjoy carving your pumpkins while you can because by the time your children are in grade school they will probably take over the responsibility . . . and the fun of it. Never carve a pumpkin more than two days before Halloween.

Or better yet decorate your pumpkins with permanent markers and use them for cooking on or after Halloween. Use a cleaned-out pumpkin for cooking and as a serving bowl for a stew.

Or simply cook up the pumpkin for a vegetable dish or for pumpkin cake:
　　　　Wash pumpkin; cut into large pieces. Remove the seeds and strings or fibers. Put pumpkin pieces,

(continued on next page)

shell side up, in a baking pan and bake in a 325 degree oven for 1 hour or more until pumpkin is very tender. Scrape pulp from the shell; put through a food mill or ricer. If the pumpkin is not thick enough to stand in peaks, simmer it in a saucepan on top of the range for 5 to 10 minutes, stirring constantly. Freeze in amounts you would use at one time.

TOASTED PUMPKIN SEEDS

Don't throw away those wet, string-laden seeds from your pumpkin. They are a delicious treat! Wash the seeds and remove the strings to the best of your ability. Let the seeds soak in salted water over night. (1½ tsp. salt per ⅔ cup water.) Then place the seeds in a low baking pan in the oven at 300° for approximately 20 minutes or till golden. Eat with or without removing the shells.

   Of course, you can squirrel away a few seeds (not toasted) and plant them in the springtime in your garden.

PUMPKIN CUP

Cut off a "cap" of an orange, preferably navel variety. Remove the inside pulp and fill with fruit or even candy. Put a toothpick on the top of the "cap" which can be used as the eating utensil. Also, scratch a face onto the orange and go over the "face" with a ball point pen so the features stand out.

PUMPKIN MUFFINS

    1¹/₂ cups flour
    ¹/₂ cup sugar
    2 tsp. baking powder
    1 tsp. cinnamon
    ¹/₂ tsp. ginger
    ¹/₄ tsp. cloves
    ¹/₂ cup raisins
    1 egg, slightly beaten
    ¹/₂ cup milk
    ¹/₂ cup canned solid pack pumpkin
    ¹/₄ cup butter or margarine, melted
    ¹/₄ Tbsp. cinnamon-sugar

Sift together first 6 ingredients into mixing bowl. Stir in raisins. Combine egg, milk, pumpkin and melted butter. Add wet ingredients all at once to sifted mixture, mixing only until combined. Fill greased muffin pans two-thirds full; sprinkle with 2¹/₂ tsp. sugar mixed with ¹/₂ tsp. cinnamon. Bake in 400 degree oven for 20 to 25 minutes. Makes 1 dozen muffins.

DESSERT "PUMPKINS"

• Orange frosting for cakes or cupcakes is made by adding equal drops of red and yellow food coloring to white frosting.

• To make black frosting mix the following together and add it to white frosting:

    1¹/₂ tsp. green food coloring
    1¹/₂ tsp. red food coloring
    5 drops blue food coloring

• Candy corn makes good eyes, nose and mouth "face" decorations.

• Cookies too can be covered with orange frosting.

TRICK OR TREAT

There will be plenty of candy given out in your
neighborhood. For the sake of maybe just one less
cavity for some family somewhere, why not consider
giving out one of the following:

> Sugarless bubblegum
> Sugarless gum
> Apples
> Popcorn
> Small bags of pretzels or potato chips
> Peanuts in shell
> Any variety of nuts, shelled or not

P.S. This is probably the one night you should
make *sure* the kids brush their teeth.

Also keep in mind that "make-up" is just as much
fun, and a good deal safer than wearing a face mask
on Halloween night.

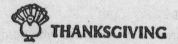 **THANKSGIVING**

This warm, family holiday centers around a large
turkey dinner which most children thoroughly
enjoy.

CANDIED CRANBERRIES

This festive holiday snack gives the older toddler
who wants to "help" a chance to do so.

> 2 cups fresh firm cranberries
> 4 cups sugar
> pinch of cream of tartar
> 1 cup water

Wash berries and dry on a towel. With a small
skewer or heavy blunt pin, prick each berry

through . . . this is where your toddler comes in. Combine 3 cups sugar, 1 cup water, and a pinch of cream of tartar in a 2-3 quart saucepan and cook over medium heat until it reaches 234° (soft ball stage) on a candy thermometer. Remove from heat and pour in cranberries and stir gently to coat each berry. Let stand at room temperature for at least 12 hours.

Then bring cranberries to a simmer over medium heat, stirring occasionally. Drain berries in a sieve over a bowl and put syrup back on the heat. Bring to a boil and boil rapidly to hard ball stage (250°). Remove from heat and drop in cranberries. Coat with syrup. Lift berries out with a slotted spoon and cool on waxed paper. If a pool of syrup forms around the berry, lift it to a clean spot. When cool, roll a few at a time in the remaining sugar. Leftover syrup can be used over ice cream or for candied fruit.

PUMPKIN DESSERT CAKE

Children are seldom delighted with pumpkin pie. This recipe lets you have your traditional pumpkin dessert, but in a form your children will love.

1¼ cups oil
4 tsp. vanilla
1 cup honey
1 cup molasses or sugar
4 eggs
2 cups pumpkin or one (15 oz.) can of pumpkin
½ cup wheat germ
2 cups whole wheat flour
1½ cups white flour
2 tsp. baking soda
2 Tbsp. cinnamon
1 Tbsp. nutmeg
2 tsp. ginger
2 tsp. ground cloves

(continued on next page)

Combine the first six ingredients and mix well.
Combine the dry ingredients, mix well then combine
with wet ingredients. Mix till blended. Grease two
bread pans and bake at 350 degrees for one hour.
Or in a large, low rectangular pan for 35 minutes.
      You can also make drop cookies from this
batter. Bake them at 350 degrees for 10 minutes.

And to top off this cake, try the following **Cream
Cheese Frosting:**

> 3 oz. cream cheese
> 6 Tbsp. butter or margarine
> 1 tsp. vanilla
> 1 Tbsp. milk
> 2 cups powdered sugar

Mix above, and spread on cooled cake or cookies.
Extra frosting makes an excellent filler between
two graham crackers.

APPLE TURKEYS

Use apples as the "body." Use "tail feathers" cut
from orange peels and attached with toothpicks
to the apple. Cut the head and feet from heavy
paper with toothpicks held on to paper with tape.

Take advantage of what is right outside your door:

ICE CREAM SNOW

1 cup milk
1 egg, beaten
½ cup sugar
1 tsp. vanilla

Blend the above well and add clean, fresh snow till absorbed. (May not be advisable in poor-air-quality areas.)

Maple Snow Ices: Pour maple syrup over a cup full of snow

or

make your "Maple" syrup by boiling 1 cup of water; lower heat and add 2½ cups of packed brown sugar. Heat will dissolve the sugar. Add 1 tsp. maple flavoring. Remove from the heat and add ½ cup light corn syrup. Makes 2 cups. Store in the refrigerator.

or

Orange Slush: Spoon some thawed orange juice concentrate over a dish of snow.

A Winter Reminder: When you find some room in your freezer, pack away some clean snow in a plastic bag to use come July . . . either for snow cones or for a mini-snow ball fight!

Christmas Time

Here are some decorating ideas that emanate from your kitchen:

- To hang cookies on a tree, use a plastic straw and push it into a hot cookie removed from the oven and twist out a hole at the top for a ribbon to go through.

- Popcorn for stringing should be allowed to stand until it loses its crispness to make your work easier. Popcorn can also be "dyed" by dipping it into cranberry juice, etc.
- Bells on a ribbon tied around a bread basket can add a cheery note to your table.

Festive Ideas

- Make "wreath" pancakes and serve with strawberry syrup.
- Serve cooked peas in a scooped out tomato.
- Use pointed paper cups for making lime gelatin "trees." Cut away paper when mold is firm and decorate with cream cheese.
- To make a Snack Tree, use a conical styrofoam form, cover it with green paper. Use toothpicks with vegetables and edibles, such as cheese cubes, cherry tomatoes, grapes, cauliflower, green pepper, carrot slices, etc. to cover it. Serve with a dip.
- Orange Sips: Roll an orange between your hands till soft. Use a knife and cut an "X" in the orange. Insert a porous peppermint stick into the "X" and sip away!

CHRISTMAS TREES À LA RICE KRISPIES

Using the well-known Rice Krispies marshmallow bar recipe, there are many holiday treats you can devise including mini-Christmas trees:

> 5 cups Rice Krispies
> 1/4 cup margarine or butter
> 4 cups mini-marshmallows or a 6-10 oz. bag of regular marshmallows
> 10-12 regular size marshmallows and toothpicks
> green food coloring
> red cinnamon candies

Melt margarine in a 3-qt. saucepan, then add 4 cups marshmallows and cook over low heat stirring constantly till syrupy. Remove from heat, add green food coloring till a fairly dark green color. Add cereal and stir until well coated. Shape into conical forms with buttered hands. When cooled, stick a toothpick through a marshmallow and stick into the bottom to serve as the tree's base. Decorate with red candies.

Variations on Rice Krispies holiday ideas:

Snowman — 3 balls of decreasing size, rolled in coconut, stacked and decorated.

Balls — Shape around a nut or date, then roll in decors.

Pops — Shape an oval around a wooden pop stick.

Tarts — Press into a buttered muffin tin to form a tart shell to fill with fresh fruit or ice cream.

GINGERBREAD HOUSE

This is one of those nifty ideas that will really delight your kids regardless of the fact that it lacks greatly in the nutrition department. Fortunately, it's more for looking than for eating. This is a super simplified recipe that does not take a great deal of time.

To one Gingerbread Mix, add 1/3 cup water. Mix well and roll out into 1/2" thickness. It will work best if you take the time to make a cardboard pattern, but for a guideline, the base of the house will be about 4"x6" and 3½" high to the eave line. You will need six sections:

(continued on next page)

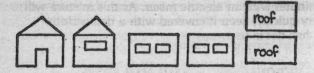

Cut the door and windows before baking, but do
not remove pieces until after baking. Extra dough
can be molded into little cookie people. Bake on
a greased sheet for maximum hardness, but without
allowing the edges to get burnt (approximately 15
minutes). The house is "glued" together with
Frosting Cement. Use toothpicks when or where
necessary. Use the Frosting Cement to hold the base
of the house to the plate so that it will stand. Let
the frame dry before adding roof.

For decoration:

Snow Landscape: Sprinkle coconut around
house, or use cotton.

Roof: Spread with icing and cover with
mini-marshmallows; or coconut; or sprinkles; or
decors; or candied fruit slices, halved.

Path: A group of any small circle candies such
as M&M's or lifesavers, or sliced gum drops, etc.

Chimney: A pile of 2 or 3 hard circle candies or
sugar cubes cemented with frosting.

Trees: Green gum drops; lollys; pine cones or
inverted sugar cones; tree cookies.

Snow Men: From leftover frosting — shape 2
balls and let dry. Attach with frosting.

Frosting Cement . . . a smooth, hard drying
icing.

Beat two egg whites stiff with ½ tsp. cream of
tartar. Add 2 cups powdered sugar and beat 5

minutes with an electric mixer. As this mixture will dry quickly, keep it covered with a damp cloth when not in use.

TRADITIONAL GINGERBREAD MAN RECIPE

2/3 cup butter or margarine
1/2 cup sugar
2 tsp. ginger
1 tsp. cinnamon
1/2 tsp. nutmeg
1 unbeaten egg
3/4 cup molasses
3 cups sifted all-purpose flour
1/2 tsp. baking powder
1 tsp. soda
Raisins

Put shortening, sugar, spices and egg in a large mixer bowl. Mix until well blended. Add molasses and mix well. Sift together flour, baking powder and soda. Stir into shortening mixture and mix well. Refrigerate at least two hours for easier handling.

Roll out on floured board and cut gingerbread men shapes. If desired, use cut pieces of raisin for eyes, nose and buttons. Sprinkle with granulated sugar, if desired. Bake on greased cookie sheets at 375 degrees for 8 to 10 minutes. Makes about one dozen 5 inch gingerbread men.

 **SPRING**

The first inkling of spring is the celebration of **Valentine's Day**. It is a day to make good use of your heart-shaped cookie cutter . . . for breakfast toast, lunch sandwiches, cheese slices, on red Finger Jell-O, and of course, for cookies.

VALENTINE KRISPIES

Use the Rice Krispies marshmallow bar recipe
(see "Christmas Trees" on page 102), add red food
coloring to the syrup just before mixing it with
the dry cereal. Then mold it into a greased
heart-shaped cookie cutter, take it out and put it
on a plate to cool.

Need a heart-shaped cake pan,
but have no such pan?
Bake a round and a square
layer cake and combine
them like so:

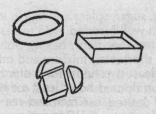

 **EASTER TIME**

This is the time of the year when the egg is used
symbolically as part of the Easter and Passover
celebrations. The egg symbolizes new life in both
traditions.

DECORATING EASTER EGGS

Do use hard-boiled eggs as they take best the stress which they are subjected to around small children. Take advantage of your own food coloring in the pantry. Let your eggs soak for at least half an hour in bowls of hot water with different colors in each. After they are removed, let them dry and decorate them with non-toxic magic markers. It's a great medium and easy for the kids to handle. An egg carton or a paper roll cut into sections is an excellent drying and decorating stand. When finished, put a drop of shortening on your hands and rub over each egg to give it a shine and set the color. You can also make "glued on" additions such as ribbon, rick-rack, etc.

JELL-O EGGS

Save egg shells (either blown-out ones or half shells), rinse and let stand at least a day. Fill with Finger Jell-O (page 40). Crack and remove shell after Jell-O has hardened. Regular recipe Jell-O can be used here, just use ½ cup less of the cold water called for per 3 oz. package.

EGG TREE

A branch can be decorated attractively using decorated egg shells. Here it is necessary to blow out the inside of the raw egg before decorating and hanging. Use glue to affix strings. If a budded branch is used and put in a narrow-necked vase with water, leaves will soon adorn the branch as well as the decorated eggs.

EGG-SHAPED COOKIES

Make an egg-shaped cookie cutter by bending and shaping the open end of a 6 oz. juice can. Decorate with a variety of icings or use:

Egg Yolk Paint

Blend ¼ tsp. water with one egg yolk. Divide among several small dishes and put different food coloring into each dish. Paint designs on cookies before baking.

If you're not up to making your own dough, use a roll of refrigerated sugar cookies and shape.

BUNNY SALAD

Place a canned pear half on a bed of lettuce. Add raisins for eyes, a strawberry (with a toothpick) for the nose, toothpicks for whiskers and American cheese (or paper) for the ears.

BUNNY BISCUITS

Using refrigerated biscuits, cut one in half (horizontally) then cut one of those pieces in half to use as the head. Cut the remaining piece in half for the ears. Pinch out a bit for the tail and bake as directed.

BUNNY ICE CREAM DISH

Lay three balls of vanilla ice cream on a plate in a row . . . a large one in the center, medium size for the head and a small one for the tail. Cover with shredded coconut. Use jelly beans or almonds for the eyes and nose; paper cutouts for the ears and toothpicks or licorice string for whiskers.

BUNNY CAKES

1) Take a heart-shaped pan, bake your cake in it, cover it with white or pink frosting and decorate it like so:

paper cutouts
for ears

Jelly beans for
eyes and nose

icing or licorice
for whiskers

2) Use one layer cake pan. Cut layer in half. Put in filling of your choice and stand them side by side. Shape rabbit by cutting out notch to make a body and head. Use notch for tail. Frost with fluffy white frosting. Sprinkle with coconut. Insert paper ears. Use jelly beans for eyes, and nose and licorice for whiskers. Sprinkle green tinted coconut and more jelly beans on the cake platter.

Tinting Coconut

Add a few drops of food coloring into a small
amount of water in a bowl, and add coconut and
toss with a fork till evenly distributed.

or

toss in a small jar 1½ cups coconut with 1-2 Tbsp.
fruit flavored Jell-O and shake well.

EASTER BASKETS

- Use a pipe cleaner as a "handle" on a margarine
  tub. Fill with seedless green grapes.
- Decorate a frosted cupcake with green tinted
  coconut. Use pipe cleaners to form basket handle.

An Easter egg hunt — indoors or out — is always
great fun. Add some hidden peanuts-in-the-shell to
provide extra hunting fun. (Do keep an accurate
count of eggs hidden indoors!)

So You're Having
a Birthday Party!

Here are a few ideas and insights that may help you keep birthdays the happy days they're supposed to be.

The only "rule," and the one that is often the most impossible to follow, is:

THE NUMBER OF GUESTS SHOULD NOT
EXCEED THE NUMBER OF YEARS OF YOUR
CHILD'S AGE.

YEAR ONE:

Starting with your child's first birthday, the above
"rule" is automatically cancelled out. There is at
least one set of grandparents, an aunt, your cousin,
his uncle, the babysitter, this neighbor, that friend,
etc. This can all work out very well if you accept
the fact that this party is for the adults and not for
your child. The food can be fancy and oriented
towards the adults because your baby will care very
little about the food . . . unless s/he can get hands
into the goo or ice cream. The presents will be a
bewilderment but the attention, excitement and
picture taking will be truly enjoyed.

If you find this to be a gathering of mothers with
their small children, consider a BYOHC (Bring Your
Own High Chair) party. Provide disposable bibs,
Wash & Dries and teething biscuits as favors.

Limit the party to one hour.

YEAR TWO:

By the second year, the miracle of maturation
brings on a clear understanding of a birthday, its
food and its presents. Keep the party as small . . .
yes as small . . . as possible. Two year olds are a
bit young for games yet. A supply of toys and
balloons works well. As sharing is not usually a
strong point at this age, you may spend some time
refereeing. Odds are you'll also be entertaining the
Mommys and possibly the Daddys.

A good food idea for the children is something simple like cupcakes and/or ice cream cones with sprinkles. Disposable bibs and Wash & Dries may still be in order. The birthday cake with the candles may be for the adults, but only after its candles are blown out and the children are served their treat. Or in other words, don't waste good food on the kids — they usually don't eat more than a few bites.

Limit party to an hour or hour and a half.

YEAR THREE:

Now you are entering the realm of the more traditional birthday party. Games can now be played and enjoyed, though they must definitely be led. Keep it simple. Three to five short games should suffice. Avoid competitive games unless everyone can get a prize. A quiet game is a better finish prior to refreshments than an active one. (See list of games at end of the chapter.)

Your three year old can begin to learn the social graces. Manners won't be ideal but it is a starting point. Greeting guests, opening presents, verbalizing thanks, saying good-bye are concepts to be discussed before the party and congratulated on afterwards.

Your child should also be consulted on the guest list. S/he can help mail or deliver the invitations and help choose or frost the cake. Written thanks for presents are not necessary.

Food should again be simple. If you are dying to try an unusual form cake, don't. Form cakes are enjoyed, just don't get carried away. Most cakes are usually judged by their icing alone.

Also save yourself time and hassle by scooping
out ice cream balls ahead of time. Place them in a
cupcake paper and store in the freezer till you're
ready for them.

A fun "placecard" idea is a cookie with the child's
name written in icing from a tube. Or let each child
decorate his own plain cookie. Provide icing, a
popsicle stick and decorations such as sprinkles,
nuts, raisins, chocolate chips, coconut, etc.

Do include a "hunt" (candy, peanut or otherwise)
in your party. A party hat or small plastic bag is an
appropriate holder. Save some extra goodies in
case any child totally misses the boat.

While candy is an integral part of any party, if
you want to opt for some more nutritional treats,
consider these:

> raisins & nuts & sunflower seeds
> pretzels
> peanuts in shells
> fruit roll (see page 45)
> sugarless bubblegum
> finger Jell-O (see page 40)
> uncandy bars (see page 42)
> dietetic or carob covered raisins

A favorite treat that makes birthdays special is
Candy cookies, either for a party or for a birthday
snack at nursery school. By only adding the
candies to the top of the cookies and making use
of the Cornell Triple Rich Formula (see page 75)
you can compromise kids' love for candy with a
bit of nutrition.

CANDY COOKIES

1 cup oil
1 cup brown sugar, packed
$1/2$ cup sugar
2 eggs
2 tsp. vanilla
$2 1/4$ cups flour (see Triple Rich Formula)
$1 1/2$ tsp. baking soda
1 cup (or less) M&M plain chocolate candies

Cream oil, sugars, eggs and vanilla. Mix dry ingredients and combine with creamed mixture. Drop by the teaspoonful on an ungreased cookie sheet. Flatten to not more than 2" diameter. Decorate with 4-6 candies per cookie but do make sure, to avoid being hassled, that the number of candies IS THE SAME FOR EVERY COOKIE.

Bake at 375° for 8-10 minutes. After baking, it is common for the candies to crack. This recipe makes from 2 to 4 dozen cookies depending on the size of your teaspoonful.

We can offer no advice on presents, prizes or party favors. You alone must live with your budget and your neighbors. But do remember, **more does not mean better.**

Limit the party to one hour and a half.

YEAR FOUR:

Most of what goes for a three year old's party is applicable here and more so. By now, the Moms and Dads are no longer on the side lines so it's up to Mom (or whomever) to keep the ball rolling.

If you find being the leader, songmistress, photographer, waitress, clean-up committee, etc. too much for you, have someone help you . . . even a neighborhood teenager.

To help alleviate the initial awkwardness of the party's start while waiting for all the guests to arrive, plan some activity such as stringing a birthday necklace, decorating a "favor" bag, or even opening the presents.

Games are eagerly anticipated by four year olds. A variety is good for their short attention span. (See list at end of chapter.) In addition to some games, a clown or puppet show would be a treat. Check the talent of some of the older children in your neighborhood.

You may find yourself making the party around lunch or dinner. The following is a list of foods with the best chance of being eaten:

Hot dogs (or corn dogs on stick)	Carrot sticks
	Potato chips
American grilled cheese	Dill pickles
Pizza	Apple wedges
Macaroni/cheese	Mandarin oranges
Hamburgers	Green grapes
Peanut butter & jelly sandwich (cut with cookie cutter)	(seedless)

Juice (apple, pineapple, orange)   Chocolate milk

Your four year old is also bound to judge your cake by its "cover."

For a different ice cream treat, cut off the top of an orange and scoop out inside. Put in orange sherbet and freeze until ready to serve.

Or consider a Do-It-Yourself-Sundae, so that the children can help themselves to their favorite toppings . . . fudge, honey, maple syrup, granola, nuts, crushed pineapple, coconut, whipped cream.

Or make a clown cone. Take a scoop of ice cream and top it with a sugar cone for a hat and decorate a face on it. Reddie-Whip makes good "hair." Make ahead of time and freeze.

Do not feel you have to seat a group of children in your dining room. Any appropriate room with a vinyl tablecloth on the floor and using low tables (coffee table or card tables on books or bricks) will work just fine.

While the guests can be picked up at a specific time, returning your guests to their homes lets you end the party on your schedule.

Limit party to two hours.

YEAR FIVE:

If you've made it this far, you can now start to rely on "Betty Crocker's Parties for Children" by Lois Freeman. Or if you want to change the party routine, you might want to try a movie, a play or a slumber party with just a few of your child's friends. A hayride in summer is nifty.

Keep in mind that young children enjoy most what
they know best. This is not the age for surprise
parties. Tradition . . . the same songs, cakes,
candles and games . . .

BIRTHDAY PARTY DANGERS

Beware of:
1) little girls with long hair blowing out candles
   (hair burns).
2) children running with straws or lollypops in
   their mouths.

*A Group of Preschool Games Listed in a Progressive
Order for Younger Children (2-3) to Older
Children (4-5)*

- Ball roll: with children sitting in a circle and
  legs spread, have a ball rolled from one child
  to another.
- Tell a story: from a book with large pictures
  or from your imagination — keep it short.
- Songs: Ring-around-the-rosy; Farmer-in-the-dell;
  London Bridge; Eensy-Beensy Spider; Hokey-
  Pokey.
- Animal Parade: march around as an elephant,
  a bunny, a dog, a cat, a bird, a kangaroo, etc.
- Pin the Tail on the Donkey; or the nose on
  the clown or whatever.
- Drop (or toss) a bean bag into a basket.
- Simple Simon . . . and keep it simple.
- Balloon push: outside it can be done with a kick,
  inside crawling and using one's nose.
- Kangaroo race: hop holding a balloon between
  knees.
- Ring the bell: throw a bean bag or Nerf ball
  at a bell . . . hanging in a tree outside or a
  doorway inside . . . so it will ring when hit.

- Musical chairs: the way you remember it or a variation . . . passing a plastic or tin plate, the holder when the music stops is "out."
- Dress up: have a large pile of oversized clothes, hats, shoes, etc. that they all race to get into simultaneously (take photos).
- Duck Duck Grey Duck: a circle game of catch.
- Doggie, Doggie, Who's Got the Bone? Children sit in a circle, one in the center is blindfolded and an object is given to one child, then all children put their hands behind their back and the group recites, "Doggie, Doggie . . ." With blindfold off, the child now is given the 3 chances to guess who has the "bone."
- Shoe race: everyone removes shoes and places them in a pile, then on signal they race to find and put on their own shoes (forgo buckling and tying) and race to a finish line.
- Bingo!

Kitchen Crafts

Work and play are not separate in a child's world. They are inseparable, and the same in relation to you — you work and they play. Your time is often spent in the kitchen and so will your child's. So give him/her a chance to do some creative "messing around"!

First there is the kitchen itself with all the grown-up tasks to be done. Many of these can be shared with your youngsters. Don't expect perfection. Remember they are new to these tasks.

a) Washing dishes . . . either dirty or just extraneous ones.
b) Setting the table.

c) Folding napkins.
d) Washing and cleaning vegetables.
e) Scrubbing the floor.
f) Cleaning your kitchen sink . . . it will be
   spotless, at least in some spots.

Your kitchen can also serve as the starting place
for many fun activities. If you've never made your
own play dough, now is the time to start. We've
listed three recipes, each with special characteristics.
Experiment to find your favorite. Age may also
determine which you'll use.

#1 PLAY DOUGH (no-cooking recipe)

Mix:

  1 cup white flour
  $1/2$ cup salt
  2 Tbsp. vegetable oil
  1 tsp. alum (if you can't find it at the grocery store,
    it is available at the drugstore.)

Add a small amount of water at a time until
consistency of bread dough. It will not be more
than $1/2$ cup. Add food coloring, preferably to the
water before mixing. You can make colors not
available, such as purple, by creatively mixing colors.
Store in an airtight container or plastic bag. It lasts
a long time.

#2 PLAY DOUGH A LA PEANUT BUTTER

Mix:

  1 jar of peanut butter (18 oz.)
  6 Tbsp. honey
  non-fat dry milk or milk plus flour to the right
    consistency
  Optional: cocoa or carob for chocolate flavor

Shape . . . Decorate (raisins?) . . . and Edible!

#3 PLAY DOUGH (stove-top recipe)

Mix in a medium pot:
  1 cup white flour
  ¼ cup salt
  2 Tbsp. cream of tartar

Combine and add:

  1 cup water
  2 tsp. vegetable food coloring
  1 Tbsp. oil

Cook over medium heat and stir (about 3-5 minutes).
It will look like a "globby" mess and you'll be sure
it's not turning out . . . but it will. When it forms
a ball in the center of the pot turn out and knead
on a lightly floured surface. Store in an airtight
container or plastic bag. Edible but not as tasty as
recipe #2!

When using play dough, don't neglect those
necessary pieces of equipment: cookie cutters,
rolling pins (real or play), plastic knives, bottle caps,
extra flour, uncooked spaghetti or macaroni,
walnut half-shells, etc.

When your child is old enough to appreciate
something a bit more lasting, add "real" homemade
clay to your bag of tricks.

CLAY FOR PLAY AND POSTERITY (baking method)

Mix: 1 cup salt
    ½ cup water
    2 Tbsp. vegetable oil
Add: 2 cups flour

After shaping, the clay can be baked at 250 degrees
for several hours.

CLAY FOR PLAY AND POSTERITY
(overnight drying methods)

Mix: 1 cup cornstarch
     2 cups baking soda (1 lb.)
     1¼ cups cold water

Stir in a saucepan over medium heat for about 4 minutes until the mixture thickens to moist mashed potato consistency. Remove from the heat, turn out onto a plate and cover with a damp cloth till cool. Knead as you would dough. Shape as desired or store in airtight container or plastic bag.

    For color, add a few drops of food coloring to the water before it is mixed with starch and soda. Or objects may be left to dry and then painted with water (tempera) colors or acrylics. Dip in shellac or brush with clear nail polish for a sealer.

CLAY RECIPE FOR CHRISTMAS ORNAMENTS
(oven drying method)

Mix well in a large bowl:
    4 cups flour
    1 cup salt
    1 tsp. powdered alum
    1½ cups water

If the dough is too dry, work in another tablespoon of water with your hands.

    Dough can be colored by dividing it into several parts and kneading a drop or two of food coloring into each part. Roll or mold as desired.

    To Roll: Roll dough ⅛" thick on lightly floured board. Cut with cookie cutters dipped in flour.

(continued on next page)

Make a hole in the top, ¼ inch down, for hanging,
by using the end of a plastic straw dipped in
flour. Shake the dots of clay from the straw and
press on as decorations.

To Mold: Shape dough no more than ½" thick
into figures such as flowers, fruits, animals, etc.
Insert a fine wire in each for hanging.

Bake ornaments on ungreased cookie sheet for
about 30 minutes in a 250° oven. Turn and bake
another 1½ hours till hard and dry. Remove and
cool. When done, sand lightly with fine sandpaper
till smooth. Paint with plastic-based poster, acrylic
paint or markers. Paint both sides. Allow paint to
dry and seal with clear shellac, spray plastic or
clear nail polish.

This recipe makes about 5 dozen 2½"
ornaments.

CLAY RECIPE FOR "COOKIE" ORNAMENTS
(overnight drying methods)

Mix:
> 2 cups salt
> ⅔ cup water

Stir and boil.

Add:
> 1 cup cornstarch
> ½ cup cold water

Stir. If it doesn't get thick, set back on the stove.
Use extra cornstarch on table and rolling pin.
Roll out dough and cut with cookie cutters. Use
straw for making hole at the top for hanging.
Dry and decorate. Use paint, glitter, etc. Remember,
these are not edible!

BREAD CLAY RECIPE

Whoever said that plain old white bread isn't worth anything! Just remove the crusts from 6 pieces of white bread and knead them with 6 Tbsp. of white glue plus either 1/2 tsp. detergent or 2 tsp. glycerine. Knead mixture till it becomes nonsticky. Separate into portions and tint with food coloring. Shape and when done, brush with equal parts glue and water for a smooth appearance. Let dry overnight to harden. Paint which will seal and preserve would be acrylic paints or plastic spray. Or use clear nail polish.

HOMEMADE "SILLY PUTTY"

Mix well:
> 2 parts white glue (Elmer's)
> 1 part Sta-Flo liquid starch

It needs to dry a bit before it is "workable." It may be necessary to add a touch more glue or starch. You will have to experiment. It may not work well on a humid day. Store in airtight container.

Note: If you use Elmer's School Glue instead of regular white it doesn't bounce or pickup pictures, but it makes a gooey delight your kids will love. Use on a smooth surface.

Homemade "Silly Putty" has the same nasty characteristics of commercial Silly Putty. Beware of contact with clothes and carpet.

You will probably find yourself supporting Elmer's Company — both for their regular glue and their school (more washable) glue. But home paste will work for many projects.

NO COOK PASTE

Mix:
    handful of flour

Add:
    water till gooey

Add:
    a pinch of salt

This same recipe can also be used as a quickie
finger paint concoction by adding some food
coloring and working it on heavy paper or
cardboard. Also works well as a papier mâché paste.

LIBRARY PASTE

Mix in a saucepan:
    1 cup flour
    1 cup sugar
    1 tsp. alum
    4 cups water

Cook until clear and thick. Add 30 drops oil of
cloves and store covered.

LIGHTWEIGHT GLUE

Egg white makes a good adhesive to glue the paper
of kites. It is strong and almost weightless.

FINGER PAINTS

Finger painting with small children does not occupy
their attention for as long as we would wish
(cleaning up always seems to take longer than
play time) but it's worth the effort for the discovery

and fun value. Do not "show" your child how to use finger paints as you think they should be used. The adventure is the best part. Sometimes, it will be fun for him/her just to feel the cool, smooth paint and see the bright colors.

#1 FINGER PAINTS

3 Tbsp. sugar
1/2 cup cornstarch
2 cups cold water
food coloring

Mix the first two ingredients and then add the water. Cook over a low heat, stirring constantly, until well blended. Divide the mixture into 4 or 5 portions and add a different food coloring to each, plus a pinch of detergent. The latter facilitates cleaning up.

#2 FINGER PAINTS

1/2 cup dry laundry starch
1/4 cup cold water
1 1/2 cups boiling water
1/2 cup soap flakes
1 tsp. glycerine
food coloring

Mix starch and cold water in a saucepan. Pour in the boiling water and cook over low heat till shiny. Remove from the heat and add soap and glycerine. Divide the portions and add different food coloring.

Variation: Just beat warm water into Lux or Ivory Flakes till consistency desired and add paint or food coloring.

(continued on next page)

If you don't wish to go to the "trouble" to mix
finger paints, add a drop of food coloring to aerosol
shaving soap and let your child do his/her thing
on a cookie sheet.

Regarding regular water-based paint, a good
investment is powdered poster paint which can be
found in an art supply or crafts store.

Brushes: Try a pastry brush if you can spare yours.
These have wider handles and the less flexible brush
cuts down on splatters.
    Or try cotton swabs. A swab can be used for
each color so that paint (hopefully) remains unmixed
and bright.

The floor (if not carpeted) covered with newspapers
is often the best painting place since it often has
to be cleaned after a painting session anyway!

PRINTING

Printing — Vegetable Style

Use a potato, carrot or turnip cut in half, carve
out a raised design (mom's job) and then dip a
brush into some poster paints (or use an ink pad)
to cover the design. Press down firmly on paper —
white tissue paper, uncoated shelf paper, ribbons,
etc. Let dry.

Also making lovely prints are sliced citrus fruits,
apples, and even onions.

Printing — Kitchen Utensils

While sponges, plain or cut into shapes, are the
most obvious item to use for printing, remember
to try some of the following: a potato masher,
wooden salad fork, extract bottle bottoms,
toothbrushes, etc.

Stained Glass Crayons

A good way to make use of all of those broken
crayon pieces (of which there always seems to be
an over supply) is to make stained glass crayons.
Simply remove any covering paper and place the
pieces in a well greased muffin tin (or use tin foil in
each muffin section) and put in a 400° oven for a
few minutes till melted. Remove from the oven
and cool completely before removing from tin.
If you mix the crayon colors, the circles will have a
lovely stained glass effect and are great fun to
color with.

Peanut Butter Bird Feeder

Take a pine cone and spread peanut butter on each
"leaf." Roll this in a dish of bird seed. Use a piece
of yarn or wire to hang it from a tree.

Chase the Pepper

You don't have to understand the scientific principle
to be entertained by this magic trick illustrated on
p. 130.

Fill a pie plate (or small sink) with water. Shake
pepper on the water. Take a piece of wet soap and
dip it into the water. The pepper will run away
from the soap. Now shake some sugar into the
clear area and the pepper will run back.

Bean Bags

Bean bags were more plentiful when dried beans
were lower in price. Every toy chest still needs a
few. Sew three sides of two fabric squares together;
add beans and sew fourth side. Or use a small
child's orphaned sock or mitten as a bean bag.
Sew up!

Crystal Garden

Mix: 4 Tbsp. salt
      4 Tbsp. water
      1 Tbsp. ammonia

Pour this mixture over several small pieces of
charcoal in a small bowl. Put several drops of
different colored inks on various parts of it. Leave
this undisturbed for several days and crystals will
cover it in an interesting formation, growing and
spreading every day. It will be white where no
ink is used.

PARAPHERNALIA FROM PAPER
PRODUCTS

Here are just a few ideas for using those items
surrounding us:

Straws

To make any day special, and maybe to encourage
the drinking of an unfavorite beverage, try this
trick. Make a cutout (one paper plate will provide
a whole batch) in a circle or special shape and
use a hole puncher to make a hole in the top and
bottom of your design. Decorate or let your child
do so, then weave the straw in the one hole and
out the other. By using names on your design
these could serve as "place cards" for a birthday
party.

Milk Cartons

Of the many things you can do with your empty
wax milk cartons, consider this one.

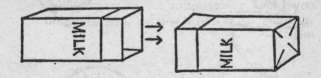

Building Blocks: Using two of the same size milk
cartons, open up the top ends completely, then
slide them together as shown to make a block.
Cover with Contact, etc.

Paper Cups

These can be made into:
1) bells (decorate)
2) a minidrum by covering with paper held in place by an elastic.
3) a telephone when two are connected with a long string.
4) spyglasses when two are attached with tape, holes punched out for eyes and by using string to go around the head.

PAPER PLATES

These can be used:

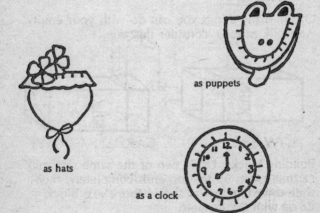

as puppets

as hats

as a clock

Paper Bags — Brown Variety

Large brown paper bags make good life-size masks and costumes for a young child. Help them cut out facial features and the room for the arms and then let them do the rest.

Brown bags can also be decorated even when to be used as garbage bags.

A smaller bag makes an excellent hand puppet. Make the "head" on the base of the bag.

A flashlight face can be made by cutting out features on the base of a bag, inserting the flashlight inside, then twisting the bag around the handle using tape to hold it while leaving an opening for the switch.

Or a tote-bag:

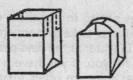

HOW DOES YOUR GARDEN GROW?

There are several easily grown items that may be of special winter time delight for your child as s/he can do all the work.

A good functional container is a cut-down milk carton with potting soil and holes punched in the bottom for drainage. Or you may even want to use a half egg shell. A ¾ egg shell decorated makes a delightful pot or better yet it can be a "head" with anything green grown for its "hair." Place "pot" in a sunny or well-lit window.

Cress: This is easy to grow and can even be added to salads a few weeks after planting.

Dried Beans:* Roll a piece of paper towel into a clear glass. Put a bean between the paper and the side of the glass. Keep it moist. You can watch the seed send roots down and sprouts up.

Citrus Seeds: Cover 4 or 5 seeds (orange, lemon or grapefruit) in a container and cover with ½ inch of soil. Keep soil moist by gently covering with clear wrap till they have germinated.

Things to place in water for fast growth or root development:

1) A large sweet potato in a shallow dish should have enough water to keep it covered. Keep it half covered in water as the days pass. It will grow a lovely vine for you. If you have no luck, try a new potato as they are often treated to prevent growth.
2) Carrot tops (top few inches) that *you* have cut off the green tops from, will sprout again if left in water.

---

* Lima or corn kernels, etc.

3) Place grass seed or bird seed on a sponge which is wet and placed in a shallow dish. Let the saucer always show a little water so that you know the sponge has not dried out. Your child can "mow the lawn" if s/he can handle a scissors.

Though the avocado pit is a popular item to grow, it is not much fun for small children as germination is often very slow.

Pot-Pourri

... or I Wish I'd Thought of That

This final chapter is sort of a pot-pourri — a
collection of everything that didn't fit anyplace
else. It contains many well used ideas passed from
"practicing" parents to other new parents as
practical information collected in one place for
your reference.

Peanut butter is a staple in most homes with young children. A few additions can make those sandwiches more imaginative and nutritious. Do purchase those brands in the refrigerated section of your grocery store if possible, as the unhydrogenated oil vs. shelf-stable oil is better for you. At least check the ingredients on the shelf-stable ones if that is where you're making your purchase.

1) Peanut butter and ground raisins mixed with fruit juice.
2) Peanut butter and grated raw carrots.
3) Peanut butter topped with applesauce.
4) Peanut butter topped with Baco's plus honey.
5) Peanut butter and banana slices.
6) Peanut butter and cream cheese blended plus 2 Tbsp. orange juice or honey.

Other ideas for a quick and nutritious sandwich for both parent and child include the following:

1) Cream cheese with jelly.
2) Cream cheese with ground raisins.
3) Chopped egg, cheese and bacon.
4) Ground leftovers, eggs and pickle relish.
5) Cottage cheese with grated pineapple.
6) Cottage cheese topped with sliced hard-boiled egg.

Keeping the bread in the freezer keeps it from tearing when the peanut butter or cream cheese is spread. It takes only a few minutes for it to thaw.

APPEALING LUNCH IDEAS

Fill an empty ice cube tray with finger foods such as fresh strawberries, cheese cubes, lunch-meat, hard-cooked egg wedges, carrot sticks, etc. This can be made up early in the day and refrigerated until serving time when it will provide an interesting treat for some hard-to-please toddler.

Make colorful chains of raw carrots, zucchini or cucumbers to add interest to vegetables. Cut ¼ inch slices of vegetables and remove centers. Make one cut through the rind of one half of the rings and slip them together to form a chain.

Consider a cafeteria-style meal for your child. Picking his/her own food is a real treat!

Any hot dog can be served on a wooden ice cream stick stuck into one end of it.

For the younger set who is ready to eat corn on the cob but not digest it, slice off the tops of the kernels or slice down the middles of each row of kernels so the corn can be sucked out.

Sprinkle 1 tsp. of noodle alphabet letters and 2 tsp. of instant tapioca into ⅔ cup of boiling vegetable broth. Cook over a high heat for 3 minutes, stirring constantly. Remove from heat, stir in a dash of salt and a dot of butter.

"Making your own" lunch, sandwich, etc. often helps get a food eaten.

SOME QUICK DESSERTS

CHOCOLATE CHEESE CREAM

    1 Tbsp. cream cheese
    1 tsp. milk
    ½ tsp. sugar
    ⅛ tsp. cocoa

Beat the cheese with the milk until smooth. Then beat in the sugar and cocoa.

HOMEMADE FRESH FRUIT SHERBET

    1¼ cups fresh fruit
    1 cup sugar
    2 egg whites, beaten stiff

Cut the fruit into small pieces. Mix the fruit and
sugar well. Fold in the beaten egg whites. Put in
a freezer tray and freeze for about two hours,
stirring occasionally. Cover with wax paper until
ready to serve.

GOOD CHOCOLATE "ICE CREAM" FOR TODDLERS

    ½ can sweetened condensed milk
    1½ Tbsp. cocoa
    ½ cup regular milk

Combine ingredients and freeze for about 3 hours
in a freezer tray.

APPLE CUSTARD

    1 apple
    1 egg
    2 Tbsp. sugar

Preheat oven to 350°. Wash, peel and core apple.
Cut into very thin slices and sprinkle with sugar.
Beat the egg and fold into the apples. Put these into
a well-buttered baking dish. Bake for 30 minutes.

BANANA AND APPLE WHIP

    1 small banana
    1 small apple
    1 tsp. milk
    ¼ tsp. sugar

Wash, peel and cut apple into blender-size pieces or
grate on a grater. Add the remaining ingredients
and beat until blended. Serve immediately.

BANANA INSTANT PUDDING

>   2 ripe bananas, mashed
>   1/2 cup applesauce
>   2 Tbsp. peanut butter
>   2 Tbsp. honey

Stir till smooth and chill. Sprinkle with cinnamon or wheat germ before serving.

YOGURT SUNDAE

Put some yogurt (frozen or not) in a dish. Add fresh fruit and pour honey over the fruit. Sprinkle with granola or nuts. Top with a maraschino cherry.

NO-WORK DESSERT

Serve any fruit with separate small bowls of sour cream and brown sugar. Dip the fresh fruit into the brown sugar, then the sour cream and eat.

Nutritious Frostings

Don't tell your children that the frosting is nutritious or they'll decide it's yucky before trying it. Use this on breads and muffins, as well as cookies and cakes:

Base: Cream together —

>   2 Tbsp. soft butter or margarine
>   1/4 cup honey
>   1 tsp. vanilla

Flavorings: Add to the base and whip till smooth:

Spice Frosting: 2-3 Tbsp. milk, buttermilk or yogurt, 1 cup of powdered milk and dashes of cinnamon, nutmeg and allspice.

Banana Frosting: Mash up a banana and add to spice frosting.

Chocolate or Carob Frosting: 2-3 Tbsp. of milk, yogurt or buttermilk; ¼ cup cocoa powder or carob powder; ⅔ cup powdered milk.

Fruity Frosting: 2-3 Tbsp. fruit juice; 1 cup powdered milk; some grated orange or lemon rind or chopped raisins or dates.

You may substitute peanut butter for the butter or margarine in the base and add whatever else appeals to your family. Be sure to include the dry milk.

Or sprinkle sugar and cinnamon over a cake or cookies just as you would on toast.

More frosting ideas:

- Melt half of a 6 oz. package of chocolate chips and and ½ cup of peanut butter and spread over cookies or bars.
- Honey spread on cookies makes a good "glue" frosting for adding decors, coconut, etc.
- Though not really a frosting, a quick dusting with confectioner's sugar will give a cake or bar recipe a completed look.
- Use 1 Tbsp. thawed orange juice concentrate mixed with 1 cup of powdered sugar to make a "dribble" frosting.

OTHER GOOD THINGS TO KNOW

Extra formula, when baby graduates to milk, can be used for cooking, baking or even in coffee.

When jam and jelly jars are almost empty, pour in cold milk. Shake and serve as a fruit-flavored drink.

Fill finished pickle jars that still have liquid with carrot sticks for a new flavored snack.

Toddlers are not in favor of food hot from the stove or oven. An ice cube can bring many foods to a more edible temperature quickly.

Freeze leftover juices and syrups from canned fruits in ice cube trays. These add a perk up to lemonade or fruit punch. Or, add a stick to the cube and use it as a popsicle.

A small foil plate or paper cupcake with a hole can help catch ice cream sugar cone drippings.

Freeze extra cookie dough in clean frozen juice cans which are open at both ends. When ready to use, push out, slice and bake.

Set gelatin more quickly by substituting 1 cup ice cubes for 1 cup cold water.

Do you have a baby bottle warmer? It's ideal for melting such ingredients as chocolate or shortening.

The out-grown baby cup (with the spout) makes a good gravy container and server.

A wide-mouth steel thermos will keep baby's bottle warm.

To soften stiff plastic pants, put them in a dryer with a load of towels.

BUSY LITTLE PEOPLE MAKE SPOTS

Some tried and true methods for removing those spots that are sure to show up as your child grows:

Crayon marks can be removed from vinyl tile or linoleum by using silver polish. To remove from woodwork, rub lightly with a *dry*, soap-filled steel wool pad.

Alcohol or cleaning fluid removes prices that have been stamped on plastic items.

A few spoonfuls of soda in a quart of water cleans baby bottles, toys, freshens a diaper bag and plastic panties.

Add soda to your diaper pail to *prevent odor*.

Put soda on milk spots left on upholstery or carpet. Rub in and vacuum out. It will keep stain and odor away.

Hairspray removes *ballpoint ink* on fabrics. Spray it directly on surface and wipe away with warm sudsy water.

For bubblegum in the hair, peanut butter is a terrific remedy. Then you're just stuck with washing out the peanut butter. Milk chocolate and cold cream are also effective. On fabric, apply ice and scrape off as much as possible.

For blood stains, rinse in cold water then soak in cold water with salt before washing as usual.

Seal lower cupboards against busy fingers with Scotch Strapping Tape. It takes just a short strip to do the trick.

Urine on the rug requires fast action. Mix a solution of $1/2$ cup of vinegar with $3/4$ cup of water. Apply small amounts of this on the stain. Give the solution a few minutes to work and then sponge from the outside to the center. Blot dry with a cloth. Keep the above solution on hand so that prompt action is possible.

Variation: Another solution that has been recommended is one tablespoon of ammonia in $3/4$ cup of water. Use small amounts and blot out.

Clean stuffed toys by rubbing in corn starch; let stand briefly then brush off.

If you need to **whiten socks**, boil them in water to which a slice of lemon has been added.

Chunks of soft, stale bread rubbed over wallpaper removes finger marks.

To clean baby's silver gifts, rub a small amount of toothpaste over them with a damp cloth, then rinse clean.

For washing walls and woodwork, one cup of ammonia, ¼ cup of baking soda, and ½ cup vinegar in a gallon of warm water will clean without dulling.

For cleaning appliances and windows without film or streaks, use ¼ cup alcohol, 1 Tbsp. white vinegar and 1 Tbsp. non-sudsy ammonia. Add enough hot water to make one quart.

NOW YOU ARE M.D. — MOTHER-ON-DUTY

Motherhood, you will quickly discover, is an on-the-job paramedic training program.

First keep in mind that:

Illness is a time when all feeding schedules usually disappear. The nature of even a minor illness usually dictates that "foods" give way to "liquids." Give your child plenty to drink (that is, if vomiting is not present). Appetites make up for lost meals when good health returns.

If your doctor has recommended a *clear, liquid diet,* s/he means: popsicles, frozen orange juice on a stick, Kool-Aid, clear broth, Jell-O, fruit punches, soft drinks such as cola or ginger ale that has been allowed to go flat or . . .

FRUIT ICE

    Finely crushed ice
    Thawed, concentrated frozen fruit juice

Place ice in a cup and pour juice over it. Drink or eat as a snow cone with a spoon.

Fruit Ice is also an excellent first aid measure for cut lips, bumped mouths, etc. Along with slowing down the bleeding and keeping the swelling to a minimum, it gets your child's mind off the discomfort.

If your child won't drink the needed liquids, try putting him/her into a clean tub of water equipped with a straw!

Medicinal Miscellany

- Honey and lemon juice is a good homemade cough syrup.
- A plastic roller (hair curler) makes a good "cast" for a bruised finger.
- An ice cube will help numb an area when you need to remove a splinter.
- When removing a bandaid, rub it well with baby oil before removing to make it "ouchless."
- When learning to swallow a pill, it goes down easily in a teaspoonful of applesauce.
- Treat a bee sting quickly with a paste of baking soda and water. Meat tenderizer is also said to be beneficial.
- For diaper rash, use your hair blower to warm a sore bottom. Fresh air is the best treatment for a rampant rash.
- Immediate treatment for a burn is cold water and/or ice. For a larger burn, including sunburn, cover area with a cold wet towel.

A General Feeding Guideline to Illness' Symptoms

Sore Throat: Soothing suckers (lollypops, popsicles, orange juice on a stick, etc.), ice cream and ice.

Fever: Liquids, in whatever form they will be taken. If your child won't drink large amounts, try small amounts at frequent intervals. Sometimes a return to a bottle will increase liquid intake. (Check with your doctor on aspirin dosage.)

Vomiting: Forget food and wait as long as your child will let you till you try small amounts of liquid. One method to assure slow intake is to let him/her suck on an ice cube or crushed ice. Continue to add small amounts of liquids at gradually increasing intervals till you are sure the stomach is settled. Appropriate liquids would be de-carbonated sodas, sweetened tea and Jell-O-water (one pkg. Jell-O to one quart of water). Wait half a day before starting easy solids, such as dry crackers. If vomiting recurs, start all over from the top. (Check with your doctor if it continues into a second day.)

Diarrhea: Discontinue milk (including skim, boiled or unboiled) till symptoms disappear. Appropriate liquids, at room temperature, are: juices, de-carbonated sodas, Jell-O-water (1 pkg. to 1 cup tap water). Easy binding solid foods are: mashed potatoes, rice cereals, Jell-O, dry toast, crackers, banana, and applesauce. (Check with your doctor if your baby is under six months.)

Constipation: Lots of liquids! Water, diluted prune juice, fruit juices except for the citrus ones, fruits, and yogurt. For the very small children, add a tsp. of dark Karo syrup to milk, formula or water.

Some ideas for coaxing an ailing child back to eating when health returns:

- Offer snacks frequently to break boredom, supplement small appetites and increase intake of fluids.
- Have an "eat-where-you-want" policy.
- Try novelty eating utensils (such as toothpicks).
- Serve foods in tiny portions in muffin tins or egg cartons.
- Place fruit juice in an insulated pitcher at bedside.
- Put soup in a mug.
- Make sandwich faces and cookie cutter sandwiches.
- Indoor picnic on the floor.

Poisons . . . A Very Real Danger

DO YOU KNOW THE PHONE NUMBER OF YOUR POISON CONTROL CENTER?

My POISON CONTROL phone number is ―――――
(write it down now — not later — later may be too late).

Call the number and ask about the Mr. Yuk stickers available in your local poison prevention program.

The hand of a toddler can be quicker than the eye. Prevention is the best — the only sure cure. Do not store "poisons" in low storage areas and remember that high, safe places are no longer safe when your child can climb. Poisons include household cleaners, paints, lotions, creams, polish, bleach, but especially

ASPIRIN! (Don't get in the habit of treating
medicine like candy, because it just might be eaten
that way when you're not near.)

Other poisons can come from plants. These include
hyacinth and daffodil bulbs, a dieffenbachia plant,
the castor bean plant, lily-of-the-valley (leaves
and flowers), iris rhizomes, rhubarb leaves (cooked
or raw), wild cherries, Jack-in-the-pulpit (all parts),
etc. Acorns consumed in quantity can be poisonous.
Don't let your child chew on them.

Poisons require differing antidotes. Do not induce
vomiting if the swallowed substance is a corrosive
or petroleum product and he/she is unconscious.
Try to have the person drink water and get medical
help. If the poison is a non-corrosive substance
and the person is conscious and not convulsing,
give a drink of water and then try to induce vomiting.
But, it is always best to get medical advice before
instituting first aid. The information needed via
phone or at the hospital is the child's age, weight,
type and amount of poison and symptoms.

Lock up all your medicines. By doing so, you will
convey the attitude of precaution.

Do keep IPECAC on hand — a safe drug for inducing
vomiting, along with a bottle of activated charcoal.
Neither should be used without advice from a
poison control center, a hospital or a doctor.

Gagging

In case of gagging, lean the child forward (head
almost touching floor) and either slap the back or
squeeze your arms around the midriff to force
air sharply out of lungs. Sometimes it may be
necessary to use your fingers to dislodge the object.

WE'RE GOING ON A TRIP

As a general rule, bring along edibles that are easy on the tummy, such as, crackers, cheese, fresh fruit, juices and toast and peanut butter. Don't forget those pre-moistened clean-up packets **or** a damp wash cloth in a plastic bag. Additional ideas to consider are:

1) Unless you have a cooler with you, it is safest to throw leftovers away.
2) Water varies greatly around the country and can cause problems for a baby. A plastic jug of sterile water will assure you of uniformity and sterility.
3) For the older baby on fresh milk, thorough cleaning of bottles and nipples is all that's required since germs cannot multiply on clean, dry surfaces. Fresh milk can be purchased everywhere but do be sure that the container is sealed and states that it has been pasteurized.
4) Or if you prefer, put pre-measured powdered dry milk in a bottle and add water when needed.
5) If you're eating along the way, it's wise to arrive at a restaurant before the crowd. This usually will give you the extra service you need.
6) When traveling by plane, to relieve air pressure in the ears of young ones who don't understand the technique of swallowing, let your baby drink from his/her bottle while the older child can suck on a lollypop or chew gum.

SOME FINAL PASS ALONG IDEAS

When your child becomes an "artist" use kitchen magnets to affix pictures to your refrigerator instead of tape.

Kosher salt or corn meal can make an excellent rainy day kitchen sandbox.

A covered cake pan holds paper, pens, crayons for car traveling entertainment.

In the winter, bring in a dishpan full of snow for your child to play with.

Recycle baby food jars: use in your tool box; for rock collections; freezing small quantities; holding paints which can be set in a muffin tin to prevent spilling; a collection of baby food jar tops in a plastic container is a great treat for an 8 month old; as a small bank; as spice jars; decorated as party favors and filled with treats, etc., etc., etc.

Make odd-shaped cookie cutters by tearing off the cutting edge of a foil or wrap box and bending to shape. Join ends by notching each end of strip.

When your child reaches the age when s/he doesn't want any foods "touching," you may want to try compartmentalized plates.

Non-skid appliqués or strips made for the bathtub are ideal for baby's high chair to keep him/her from sliding down in the seat.

If you can spare a bottom drawer in the kitchen, turn it into a toy drawer. It is handy both for clean-up or for fast distraction!

If your child objects to a bib, a colorful bandana scarf will serve as one for your "cowboy" or "cowgirl."

And FINALLY, some food for thought on . . .

HOW TO BAKE A CAKE

Light the oven. Get out bowl, spoons and ingredients.
Grease the pan. Crack nuts. Remove 18 blocks and
7 toy autos from the kitchen table. Measure 2 cups
of flour. Remove Kelly's hands from the flour.
Wash flour off. Measure one more cup of flour to
replace the flour on the floor. Put the flour, baking
powder and salt in a sifter. Get the dustpan and
brush up pieces of bowl which Kelly knocked on
the floor. Get another bowl. Answer doorbell.
Return to the kitchen and remove Kelly's hands from
the bowl. Wash Kelly. Get out egg. Answer phone.
Return. Take out greased pan. Remove pinch of
salt from the pan. Look for Kelly. Get another pan
and grease it. Answer the phone. Return to the
kitchen and find Kelly. Remove the grimy hands
from the bowl. Wash off shortening. Take up greased
pan and find ¼ inch of nutshells in it. Head for
Kelly who flees, knocking bowl off the table.
Wash kitchen floor, wash the table, wash the walls,
wash the dishes.

Call the bakery.

Lie down.

— Anonymous

WEIGHTS AND MEASURES	SIZE OF CANS

3 tablespoons = 1 tablespoon   8 ounces = 1 cup
4 tablespoons = 1/4 cup   9 ounces = No. 1 flat or 1 cup
8 tablespoons = 1/2 cup   16 ounces = No. 1 tall or 2 cups
16 tablespoons = 1 cup   16 ounces = No. 303
1 cup = 8 ounces   12 ounces = No. 2 vacuum or
1 cup = 1/2 pint   1 3/4 cups
2 cups = 1 pint   20 ounces
2 pints = 1 quart   (18 oz. fluid) = No. 2 or 2 1/2 cups
4 cups = 1 quart   28 ounces = No. 2 1/2 or 3 1/2 cups
4 quarts = 1 gallon   46 ounces = No. 3 cylinder or
                                            5 3/4 cups
                               6 lbs. 10 oz. = No. 10 or 13 cups

MEASURE FOR MEASURE

1 pound flour = 4 cups
1 stick or
1/4 lb. butter = 1/2 cup
1 square chocolate = 1 oz.
14 sq. graham crackers = 1 cup fine crumbs
1 1/2 slices bread = 1 cup soft crumbs
4 oz. macaroni
(1-1 1/4 cups) = 2 1/4 cups cooked
4 oz. noodles
(1 1/2-2 cups) = 2 cups cooked
1 cup long grain rice = 3-4 cups cooked
juice of one lemon = 3 tablespoons
grated peel of 1 lemon = 1 teaspoon
juice of one orange = 1/3 cup
grated peel of 1 orange = 2 teaspoons
1 med. apple, chopped = 1 cup
1 med. banana, mashed = 1/3 cup
1 lb. American cheese
(shredded) = 4 cups
1 lb. raisins = 3 1/2 cups
1 lb. carrots = 4 med. or 6 small
3 cups shredded
2 1/2 cups diced
1 cup milk = 1/2 cup evaporated
milk plus 1/2 cup
water OR 1/3 cup dry milk
+ one cup water
1 cup sour milk = 1 tsp. vinegar
or lemon juice
plus fresh milk
to make 1 cup (let stand 5
minutes before using)

FOOD EQUIVALENTS FOR MILK

1 cup buttermilk = 1 cup milk
1 cup yogurt = 1 cup milk
1/2 cup ice cream = 1/4 cup milk
1/2 cup ice milk = 1/3 cup milk
1 cup baked custard = 1 cup milk
1 oz. (slice) Swiss cheese = 1 cup milk
1 slice Am. Proc. cheese = 1/2 cup milk
1 inch cube Cheddar cheese = 1/2 cup milk
1 cup cottage cheese (creamed) = 1/3 cup milk
2 Tbsp. cream cheese = 1 Tbsp. milk

METRICS

Liquid Measure

1 tsp. = 5 milliliters
1 Tbsp. = 15 milliliters
1 cup = 1/4 liter
1 pint = .4732 liters
1 quart = .9464 liters
1 gallon = 3.7854 liters

TO USE HONEY INSTEAD OF SUGAR WHEN BAKING

1) Use 2/3 cup of honey for each cup of sugar called for.

2) For each cup of honey that you use, deduct about 3 Tbsp. of liquid from the recipe. (This does not apply to yeast bread.) In baked goods—add 1/2 tsp. soda for every cup subbed.

3) Reduce oven temperature by about 25 degrees and bake a little longer as honey tends to make baked goods brown faster.

To use honey instead of brown sugar, use some molasses with the honey.

Food and Recipe Index

ABOUT THE AUTHORS

In April of 1974 six members of the Childbirth Education Association of Minneapolis-St. Paul got together to write a cookbook. They felt that CEA and other groups were doing a good job of helping women through childbirth, but there was a dearth of information about feeding and caring for all those healthy babies. All but one had two young children, and they felt that what they had learned would be of value to new mothers and other mothers with young children. So they decided to write a book that would contain the kind of practical, down-to-earth recipes and advice they wished they had when they brought their babies home.

Congratulations— But...

What about all those questions and problems that arrive with a new addition to the family? Here are several invaluable books for any new or expectant mother. They are filled with helpful hints for raising healthy children in a happy home. Best of luck and may all your problems be little ones!